Space for Architecture
the work of O'Donnell + Tuomey

Artifice
books on architecture

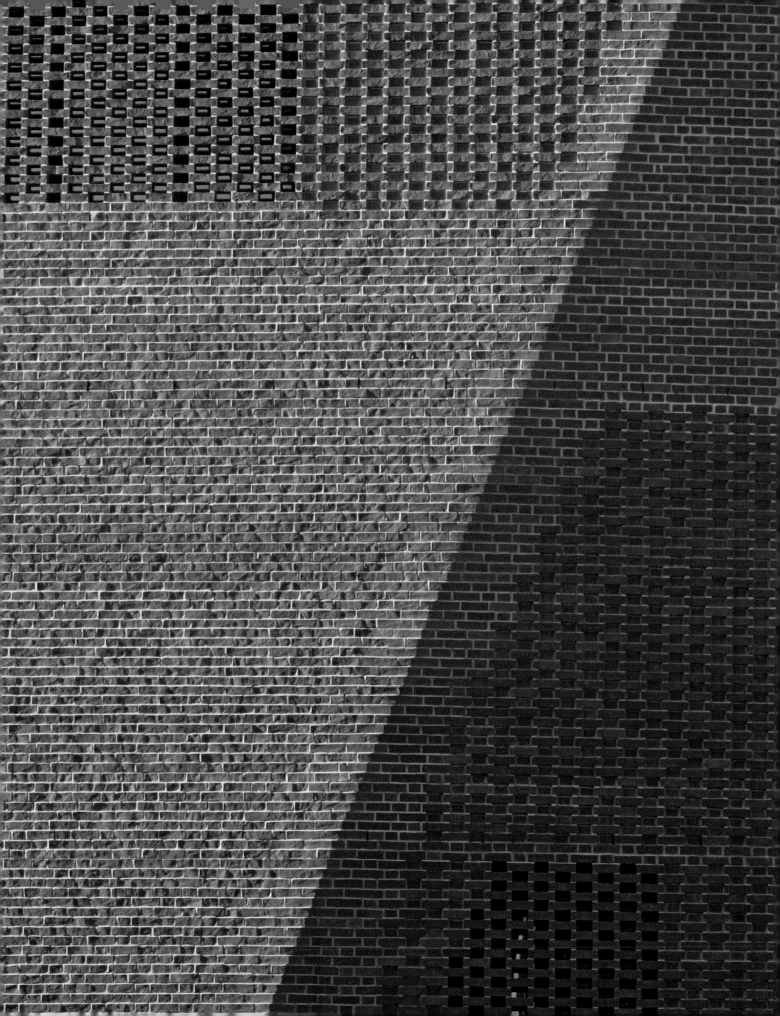

Contents

Studio Life

T he story has to start where the work starts, with the studio. In 1989 we took a long lease on a high-windowed calpstone schoolhouse, which, in previous years, had been a handbag factory, before that a sports hall and before that, a clothing warehouse. We stripped out a wooden mezzanine that cramped the space, tore up layers of lino to find a maple floor still marked out as a badminton court, cleaned the windows, painted the walls white and moved in with trestle tables, Anglepoise lamps, bentwood chairs, a circular Aalto table and six stools. This room has been our studio for 25 years, the only physical change being Willie Carey's addition of a pivoting steel framed window to improve the air on a hot summer's day and Triona Stack's installation of attic insulation to keep us from freezing in the winter. The space has steadily filled up with cardboard models, building material samples, piles of project portfolios and more and more and more files. Work stops at 11 every day for morning coffee and conversation. We work long hours. We know no weekends, as Beuys would have it.

Sheila and I sit at the back of the room, dug in furthest from the door, comfortingly surrounded by the tools of the trade: black swivel chairs (back supporting substitutes for bentwoods), ash tables, beech ply stools, Caran d'Ache clutch pencils, Swiss swivelling lead sharpeners, two kinds of scale rules, flat for measuring drawings and triangular for tearing A3 sheets off rolls of Skizzen paper. These are the conditions of studio work, the basic equipment unchanged since our student days in the 70s, the same as it was in Stirling's office in London, the same as it ever was. You sit at your desk and draw, overlaying sketches in a cumulative process of adjustment from first thought to final design. There is the insistent interruption of the telephone, the world-without-end river of worrying email, the continual distraction of client correspondence, contracts, fees and office finances. These realities cannot be denied. But this is not it. No matter how long it takes for the day's work to settle down, the defining pattern stays the same, you have to sit at your desk and draw. In between, and several times a day, you pull up a stool at a project architect's table to talk about a detail, to hear from another how things are going on site, to settle a question, to make a change, sometimes a late change, in design, or to take some suggestions back to your desk to think again. The ideal, however difficult to achieve, is a daily life of quiet routine.

Work passes back and forth from hand to hand, pencil sketches are tested out in cardboard models; changes made in freehand overlay are tried out again in hardline drawings. Computers haven't much changed the look or the meaning or the purpose of our working drawings. They speed up communication with consultants and sometimes even with contractors. Computer drawing is unforgiving in its accuracy, and this can slow down the natural quickness of early stage design, when a smudged sketch plan can be turned over into a key section in the easy blink of an eye.

Postcard pictures, of Da Messina's *St Jerome in his Study* and Vermeer's *Geographer*, are pinned on the wall above our work surfaces, stuck there to enshrine an idealised inscape of office life. The outside world would pull us in different directions, with its ceaseless demands for a person's time and attention, but the studio culture is firmly set in a deeper background and this home territory is worth defending.

OPPOSITE
Architects' studio.

ABOVE
Johannes Vermeer,
The Geographer, c. 1668.

TOP AND BOTTOM
Sheila O'Donnell; John
Tuomey in the studio.

OPPOSITE
Studio ground floor
plan, scale 1:200.

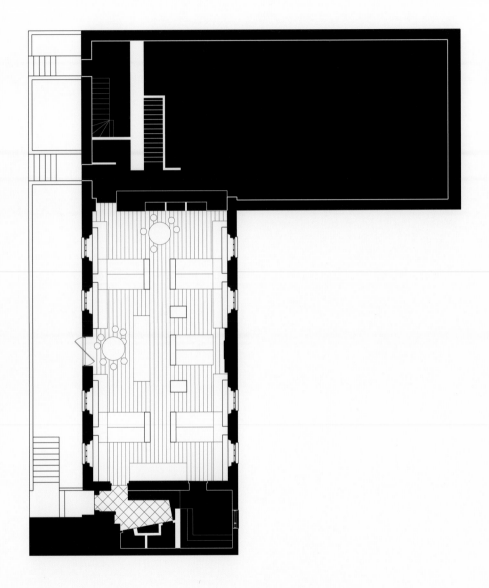

Eduardo Souto de Moura, speaking of the traditional triangle of Space Time and Architecture, says that nowadays time has become the real challenge in the working life of an architect—he complains that there is never enough time to make space for architecture.

The quick moment of conceptualisation is often quite slow in coming. False starts and dead ends can confuse the twisted path to a lateral strategy. We begin every project by a deliberate process of immersion, reading around the subject, listening to people who can help us learn something new about the given situation. Close noticing is a useful tactic, a term we have loosely borrowed from the parallel practice of creative writing. By gradual steps of observation and analysis, through

careful investigation, we prepare ourselves for the precarious, sometimes sudden and always necessary jumps in logic that lead the way to an actual architectural design. The studio provides safe ground for this otherwise unsupported activity. Many differently gifted individuals have generously contributed their skills and talents to the work of our studio. We rely completely on their dedication and diligence, their good humour and questioning intelligence, their sense of common purpose. When we talk about our work we mean to comprehensively encompass the collective endeavour of our studio. Some people stay five years; others have stayed ten, a few longer than ten. Some have moved on to set up studios for themselves. They leave their mark, their effort lives in the work, and it seems as if the room itself remembers.

LEFT
20A Camden Row.

RIGHT
The room remembers.

OPPOSITE
Books and models.

Courtyards

The following courtyard projects, by the arrangement of their plans, and for sometimes different reasons, demonstrate similar design responses to social requirements and boundary conditions. They are organised around single points of entry, turned away from the difficult conditions of the world outside, turned inwards on themselves to make a world of their own.

The school at Cherry Orchard was planned around four courtyards. Located in a socially disadvantaged suburb of Dublin, out of sight and out of mind of ordinary city amenities, the site was a treeless patch of no man's land. For a new school in this situation, vandal proof specification was regarded as an explicit and inevitable requirement of the functional design. The Department of Education took an experimental approach to this building as a pilot project, broadening the standard brief to provide for social and community activities, with multi-purpose spaces and extended hours of opening. Unlike normal practice, this school has a proper kitchen to prepare hot meals for hungry children, a pre-school nursery, early-start classrooms, a special care unit and family facilities. The intention was to provide a high quality school in a place where it was badly needed and specially designed to meet those needs.

Our approach was to convert the short term and negative expectations of the school's sponsors for night time hostility from its own daytime student population, to address the long term positive aspirations for community integration. We hoped to turn the given difficulties to collective advantage by treating the threat of vandalism as something like a climate condition. We proposed a scheme of brick walled playgrounds and gardens; an enclosed enclave built in the unbounded open space beyond the housing estates. We intended to plant each courtyard with winter flowering cherry trees. We imagined some time in the future, when the new school would have settled in and the current troubled social situation could have settled down, when it might be misremembered that the whole housing district had been named after the orchard gardens of the local community school, as if the school had been set up within an existing sheltered settlement, some sort of oasis, a social order pre-established in the bleak terrain. Cherry trees were planted at regular intervals throughout the yards and gardens, with circular cast-iron gratings around every tree and drinking fountains in each playground. Sadly, neither fruit trees nor fountains were to survive a series of changes in client management personnel. Within two years all the trees had been removed. It was decided that the tree trunks themselves were a safety hazard to schoolyard play and that every autumn would present an unacceptable seasonal danger with an uninsurable risk of injury caused by children slipping on fallen leaves. The courtyards are bare and the concept abandoned.

The building itself is built with great care and craftsmanship, with exceptional standards of brickwork and joinery. The concrete vaults, with their robustly projecting gutters, were a calculated response to the initial challenge of lessons learned from other suburban schools. We had heard worrying reports of kids climbing all over new school roofscapes, slinging slates at security men, stealing copper, and playing late night football on flat roofs in the dark.

OPPOSITE
Seán O'Casey
Community Centre,
view to tower to foyer.

ABOVE
Cherry Orchard School,
corner detail.

A happier aspect of this unusual project was the integration of a site specific and extensive sculptural installation by Janet Mullarney. Blue divers swim in the space of the vaults, an Indian cow trots up a brick pier, cloud cushions drift in front of concrete beams, flocks of sheep float by and magical dogs play. Strange ships sail through the sunlit corridors. Janet's dream figures inhabit the upper air of the school. Her optimistic menagerie inspires the children's imaginations and lifts our weary spirits.

East Wall is an inner city residential district, mostly two-storey streets of terraced housing, a surviving pocket of community life within the large scale redevelopment of Dublin's docklands. Most of the 1,800 households here would have some family history of association with the working life of the port and docks. The playwright Seán O'Casey was born in East Wall and his plays are regularly performed by the local drama group, now based in the new building. Following a short interview process, we were appointed by the docklands development authority to design a new community centre. The building, to be built on the site of a disused and dilapidated school, was to combine a number of existing social enterprises in one

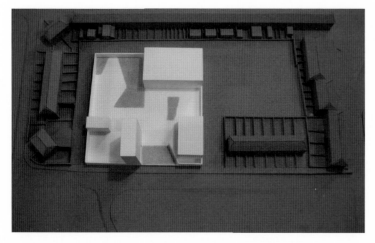

centrally administered cluster: an economic layout where locally based activities could share the benefits of belonging to a collective organism.

Our first response was to propose a single-storey courtyard-organised building to replace an existing dilapidated corridor-access school that was scheduled for demolition. Every aspect of the community brief seemed to function best at ground level; the crèche with direct access to a garden, the old people keeping an eye on the coming and going on the street, the sports hall and adjacent changing rooms adjacent to an all-weather pitch, the theatre near the front door with its backstage convenient for get-in. This simple strategy was relatively well received, and recognised as being a reasonable solution to a practical problem, but it was not enough. The building committee wanted a "big building", something that would register on the local skyline and to assert the continued presence of the community in the changed urban landscape of the docklands. This is the origin of the little stack of classrooms, with the community room at the topmost floor of

LEFT
Seán O'Casey
Community Centre,
concept model,
scale 1:500.

RIGHT
Seán O'Casey
Community Centre,
initial sketch.

the tower looking out across the houses below, to the new office blocks by the river and, away to the east, the industrial structures of the port.

We made a small white card model to show the idea of built volumes versus courtyard voids. Coloured pencil sketches described the principles and directions of the conceptual design. The building committee was representative of the various local interest groups. None of them had any experience of reading architect's drawings. They liked the idea of the gardens. All agreed that the building should feel open on the inside, not divided into rooms along corridors with closed doors like the old school. One committee member was a house painter and he spoke out strongly against any painted wall surfaces. He was aware that this was a once-off capital funded project and the community would be responsible for any long term maintenance costs.

We suggested that such an introverted scheme, focussed inwards on its own forest gardens, should indicate its identity in a different external expression. It should

not look like a house or an office or a school. It should respond to its setting in the East Wall docklands. The circular windows and corrugated concrete surfaces came out of these early conversations, with people talking about ships and silos and silent sheds. We thought of the building form as a solid block, randomly punctured across its walls and roof by holes of different diameter. The building belongs in East Wall in the same way that the Timberyard belongs in the Liberties. Both projects were designed at the same time. They take the same site-specific approach to form and character. They are visually dissimilar results of the same way of thinking. This is why they each look the way they do and not like each other. We made public presentations at evening meetings in the old school hall to communicate our proposals to the local population and to take note of their response. Architects have little to fear and plenty to learn from plain-speaking participation in situations like these. You simply say what you mean and then listen to hear whether your expressed intentions make any kind of sense in the world outside the studio.

LEFT
Seán O'Casey
Community Centre,
tower view from garden.

RIGHT
Seán O'Casey
Community Centre,
sports hall view
from garden.

+ Cherry Orchard Primary School

SCHOOL IN A WALLED GARDEN

The predominant feeling in this part of the suburb of Cherry Orchard is one of anonymity or lack of identity with public buildings subjected to considerable vandalism and hidden behind palisade fencing. The challenge was to find a design solution that would give the school a strong identity and to an extent create its own context, a context that would be welcoming and attractive for pupils from all backgrounds, including the most socially deprived.

The scheme takes the form of a school within a walled garden planted with cherry orchards. The school is arranged between a series of courtyards within a 3.6 metre high brick garden wall. The brick wall provides shelter and protection to the school and the outdoor play areas, and gives the school building a strong architectural form on the site. The rooms take their light from the courtyards, and perimeter walls are generally without openings, with the exception of the main entrance. The brick walls establish the character of the gardens. The vaulted concrete roofscape with projecting rainwater gutters reinforce the distinctive form of the building whilst deterring unauthorised access to the roofs.

The plan is a pinwheel with ranges of building opening into four courtyards. The brick-floored entrance wing contains publicly accessible facilities. This leads to the wide central school corridor/street. On each side classroom entrances are paired and recessed with shared seats. The pre-school nursery and special care unit are in a separate wing with rooms opening on each side to play areas and garden.

North playground—
walled garden.

Space for Architecture

TOP
School in a
walled garden.

BOTTOM
Waste ground site
before building.

OPPOSITE
Watercolour sketch.

　　　　　　Space for Architecture

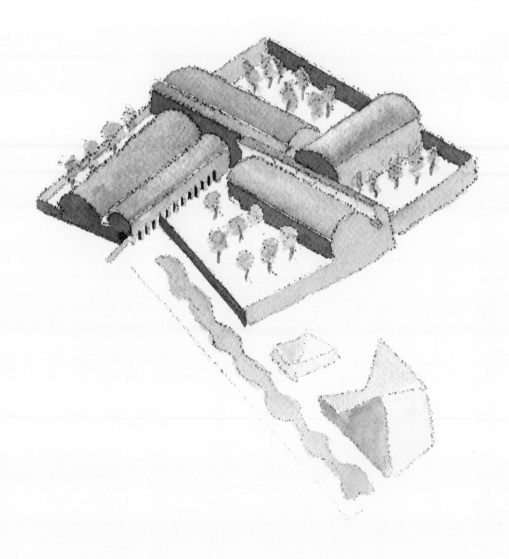

We imagined some time in the future, when the new school would have settled in and the current troubled social situation could have settled down, when it might be misremembered that the whole housing district had been named after the orchard gardens of the local community school, as if the school had been set up within an existing sheltered settlement, some sort of oasis, a social order pre-established in the bleak terrain.

Space for Architecture

LEFT
Stair detail.

OPPOSITE
Ground floor plan,
scale 1:450. School hall,
classrooms, special
care unit, four planted
playgrounds.

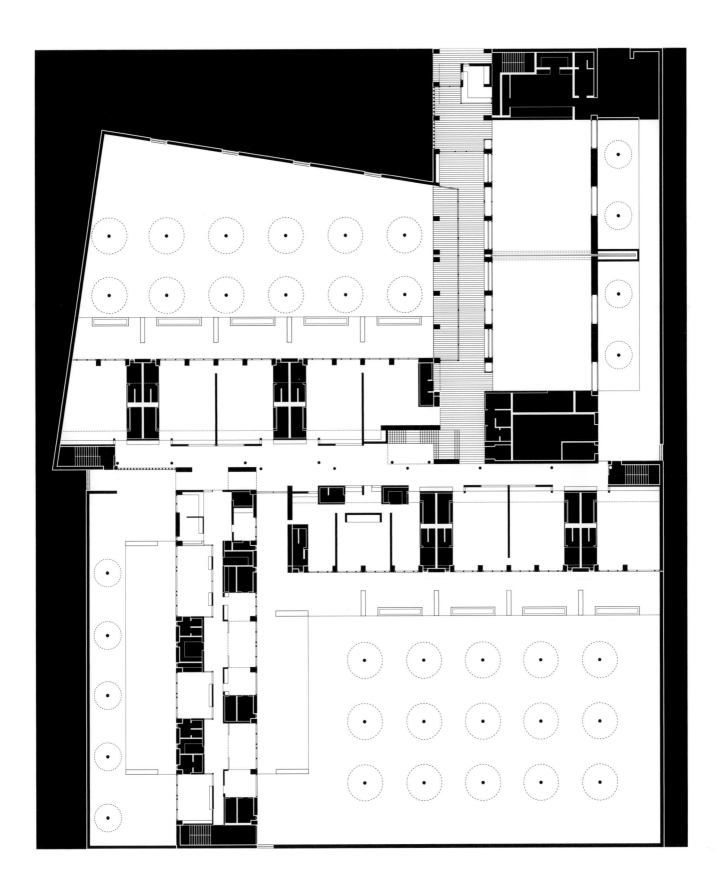

Space for Architecture

OPPOSITE
Roof detail—
concrete vault.

ABOVE
South playground—
special care unit.

Courtyards

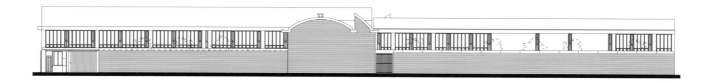

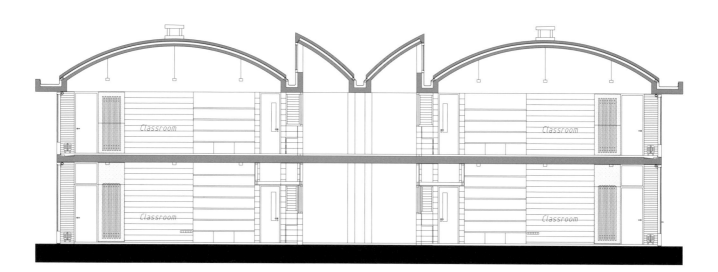

Blue divers swim in the space of the vaults, an Indian cow trots up a brick pier, cloud cushions drift in front of concrete beams, flocks of sheep float by and magical dogs play. Strange ships sail through the sunlight corridors. Janet's dream figures inhabit the upper air of the school. Her optimistic menagerie inspires the children's imaginations and lifts our weary spirits.

Space for Architecture

Courtyards   29

+ Seán O'Casey Community Centre

EAST WALL

A tight knit residential area, Dublin's East Wall nestles on a piece of reclaimed land, its perimeter defined by nineteenth century infrastructure, namely the Royal Canal and the sweep of the docklands train lines. These strong infrastructural edges define the neighbourhood's location in the city and also separate it out from the city. The community asked for a building both as a local social resource and as a representation at the city scale of their continuing presence in the changing landscape of the docklands.

A single-storey scheme answers the constraints of the programme. Four solid volumes, (tower, theatre, sports hall and plant room), are added to the plan, each representing a programmatic demand on one of the four facades, and four voids are removed from the plan, courtyard gardens providing light and ventilation to the heart of the building. The perimeter is designed as a singular uninterrupted wrapping, punctured only for communication, and scored for texture. Circular holes punctuate the facade, three sizes of window provide for standing, sitting and full-height views out of the building to the street and to the wider city. These windows act as communication devices at a larger scale, representing the community centre as a landmark, visible from the elevated train lines to the north, the sea to the east and the river to the south.

The tower gives visibility to the collective aspirations of the community centre, a symbol of its social purpose. It marks its position in its place.

The ground floor plan is subdivided in four quarters; childcare, age care, sports and drama. The quadrants overlap in the brick-carpeted common entrance hall. The four courtyards provide diagonal views and visual contact between each of the different activities.

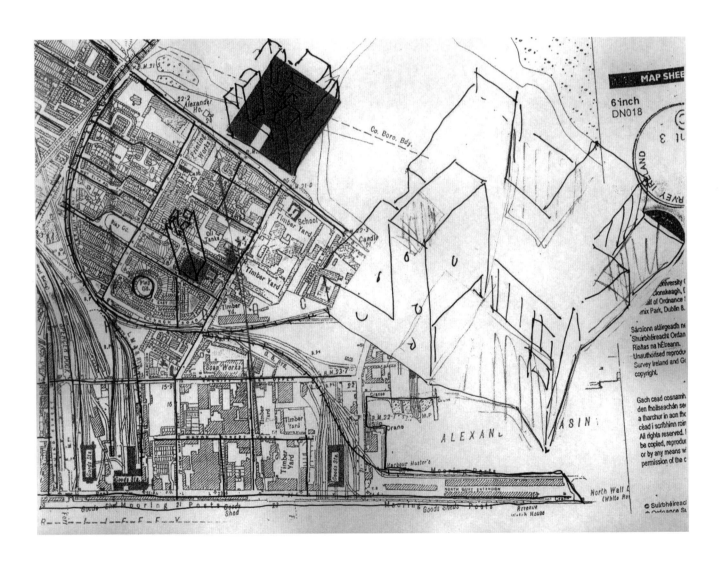

Space for Architecture

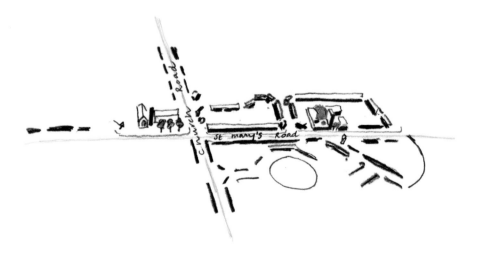

OPPOSITE TOP
The urban void, site
before building.

OPPOSITE BOTTOM
Initial sketch.

TOP
Building in context.

BOTTOM
Site sketch.

TOP
Study model, scale 1:50.

BOTTOM
Front foyer.

OPPOSITE
Forest garden.

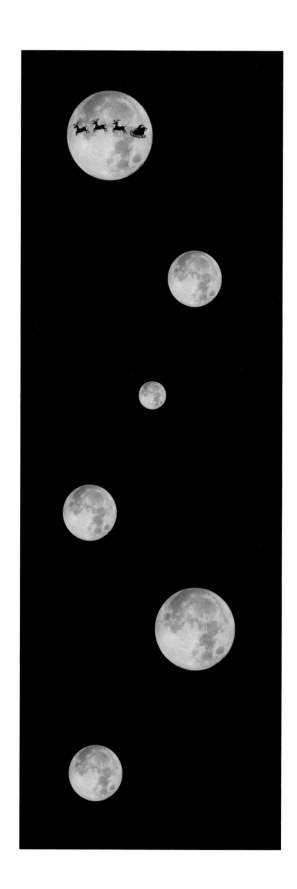

Courtyards

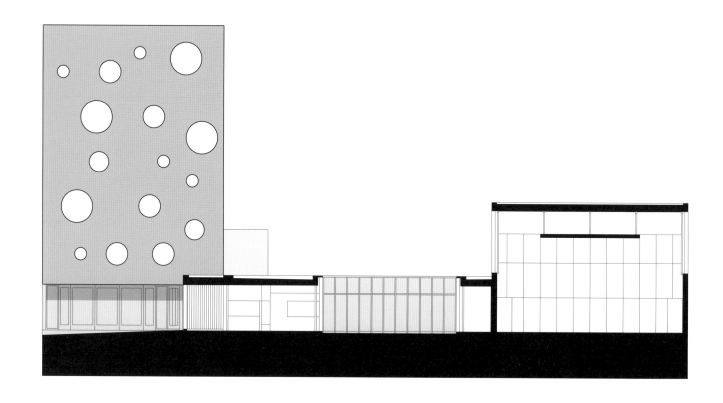

TOP
Section through
the entrance.

BOTTOM
Three women at work
in the window.

OPPOSITE
Ground floor plan,
scale 1:450. Age care,
childcare, sports hall
and performance space
around four courtyard
gardens.

OVERLEAF
Entrance hall.

Space for Architecture

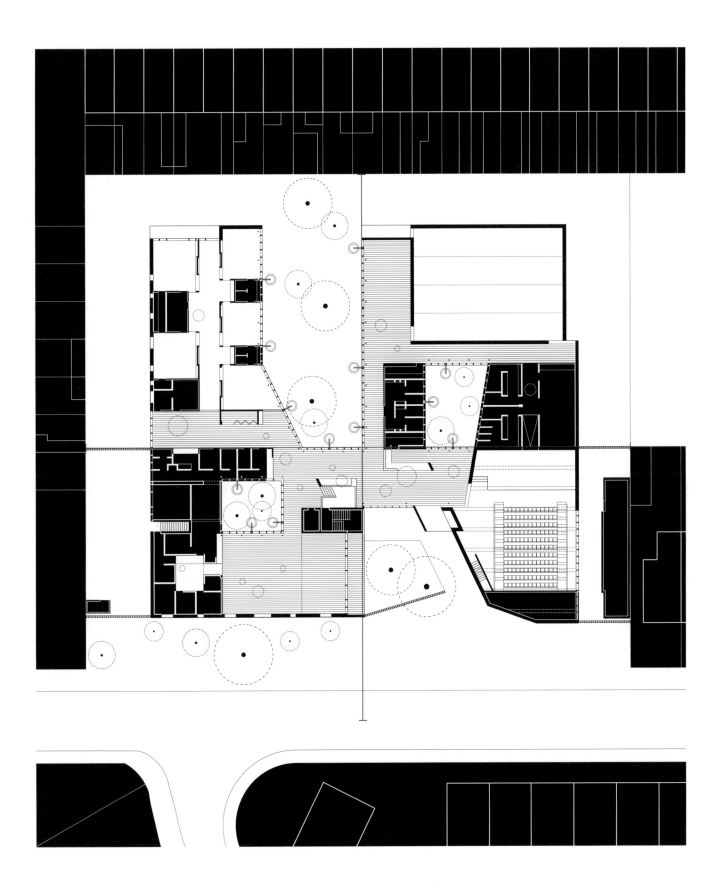

We suggested that such an introverted scheme, focussed inwards on its own forest gardens, should indicate its identity in a different external expression. It should not look like a house or an office or a school. It should respond to its setting in the East Wall docklands. The circular windows and corrugated concrete surfaces came out of these early conversations, with people talking about ships and silos and silent sheds.

The World
Outside

O ur buildings have open, permeable edges. They are not hermetic, sealed, smooth objects separated from their context or from the ground around them. They don't hover or stand in distinct contrast. They have more complex relationships with ground and air. There is an exchange between place and building, inside and outside, old and new. This phenomenon exists in time as well as place, in spirit as well as fabric.

Working on designs for schools where the brief is abrupt and basic we developed a way of thinking about the relationship between inside and outside; using intermediate, even indeterminate, spaces to prolong the experience of entering or leaving. The standard school brief has no social space; we found we could enrich the spatial catalogue by including the world outside within the orbit of the building. External

spaces that are part of the architecture but not sealed from the elements are not to be counted in the calculation of floor area. Covered verandas, steps and platforms, porches allow for some ambiguity about the state of being either inside or outside. They extend the architecture beyond the door. We are interested in contingent, even non-committal spaces, where the decision to enter can be eased or postponed.

The Ranelagh School builds its site using cut and fill to negotiate the level change on this small urban plot. The site is divided almost exactly in half between building and constructed yard. The veranda elaborates the boundary between the two conditions; the dug-in yard flows under it, staff rooms and offices project into it, and it cranks in section to define the roof terrace above. On the street side a brick wall is built hard against the boundary to protect the classrooms from the noise

OPPOSITE
Ranelagh School in context, 2014.

RIGHT
School extension, 2007.

RIGHT
Roof terrace verandah.

of passing traffic, above eye level this brick enclosure cuts back twice to provide shallow courts for light, air and outside space for the classrooms and in response to the domestic scale of the neighbouring houses.

The Hudson House, a small dwelling dug into and rising out of a narrow stepped site in the middle of Navan, was designed at the same time as Ranelagh School, and some of the same concerns were in our minds. Here the change in site level was more dramatic, the garden being a full storey higher than the street. In this house inside and outside spaces overlap, leading from an archway in the street through to the raised garden level that looks back over the town. The Hudsons ran a busy restaurant in the street-front building; the site for their new house was to be the back yard and garden behind. The yard was in the shell of a ruined shed, whose concrete walls retained the earth of the surrounding gardens. They were already living an inside-outside life. Their home was an apartment above the restaurant,

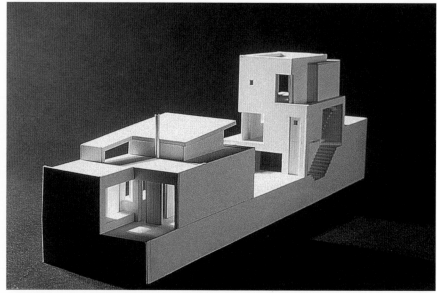

LEFT
Hudson House: cave, courtyard, tower.

RIGHT
Study model, scale 1:100.

but they took most of their meals, during breaks from the kitchen, at a table in the lovingly planted open-air ruin of the rough concrete yard. The house is built around the life they were already living in this particular place, expanded to include the rest of their domestic requirements—sleeping, reading and relaxing after work.

The plan is a rectangle divided in two and slipped. The forecourt pushes part of the living room out into the yard, creating a matching pocket space that slows and shelters the movement from living room to court. Across the court is a three-storey tower of bedrooms. There is no covered connection from living to bedrooms. Yet it is still one building; the enclosing walls and floor of the living room extend into and across the court. One wall turns up to form the gable of the bedroom tower; another runs past the tower to the raised ground beyond. The courtyard is a room in the house and a space in the town.

The house was built in three phases. First, site clearance and drainage works; second, concrete construction; third, carpentry and joinery. The concrete shell, which retains the site edges and defines the spatial enclosure, was built by a specialist contractor in a short period of six weeks. Then there was a delay before a local house-builder installed timber floors, partitions, doors and windows, to turn the structure into a house. During the pause, the distinction between inside and outside seemed unclear, the house hovered between ruin and construction, coming and going, domestic and civic. The clients held a candlelit party with hay bales for furniture, and learned to love the empty spaces of their future home.

This one-off design, which was such a particular response to its unusual site conditions and brief, has turned out to be our most generic project. Many subsequent projects have built on and developed the spatial and constructional ideas contained in this small building.

The movement through and under the Glucksman Gallery is closely related to the spatial strategy of the Hudson House. St Angela's College, currently on site, is a greatly expanded version of this world of over and under and in-between. It too is on a landlocked, steep urban site. New interventions manoeuvre their way down the hill, passing beside, between, beneath and above existing historic buildings. The scheme provides a continuous external route from top to bottom, negotiating the 18-metre drop in site levels, connecting courts, gardens and playgrounds. New buildings connect the old to each other and to the world outside. In plan it looks like a set of courtyards, but the section reveals a series of platforms, each open on its south side to the city. The social housing scheme in Richmond Hill turns the Hudson House into the hill town it always wanted to be. Galbally is a planned village set in picturesque rolling farmland. Our project extends the form of the village with two terraces of plain rendered, flat fronted houses in the tradition

**TOP LEFT AND
BOTTOM RIGHT**
Hudson House, 1998,
completed house,
concrete shell.

TOP RIGHT
Galbally social housing,
2002, porches provide
transitional space.

OPPOSITE
Glucksman Gallery,
2004, movement
through and under.

The World Outside

of Irish town buildings. Built on an incline, the roofs tilt to unify each terrace while recessed porches step up the hill to give measure and individual expression to each house. Coloured flank walls and terrazzo seats, planters and doorsteps furnish these alcoves, which provide places to pause and make a distance between private and public within the limited space standards of a social housing project.

This kind of transitional space brings the outside world into the domestic realm by framing it as a borrowed landscape, while simultaneously holding it out by means of the protective depth of enclosing walls. It acts like a zoom lens allowing the occupants to adjust their relationship with the boundaries of their domestic territory.

> A boundary is not that at which something stops, but, as the Greeks recognised, the boundary is that from which something begins its presencing.
> HEIDEGGER (QUOTED BY CHRISTIAN NORBERG-SCHULZ IN GENIUS LOCI)

In the Timberyard every apartment has a different view, each with a piece of city landscape framed from its own private terrace. Residents have an individual connection to the city beyond and they share a collective relationship with the common ground of the courtyard defined by the enclosing wall of their homes. The triangular court has a narrow opening to Cork Street, which slows and quietens the city behind. Projecting staircases, recessed alcoves, seats and trees populate this space and make it a kind of Campo—an occupied room. A slipped pattern of domestic-scaled windows suggests occupation by many people; double-height loggias mark the location of each individual apartment and give a larger scale rhythm to the facade. The brick surface steps and angles around corners to make an unbroken enclosure, starting on Cork Street, turning into the Timberyard, then crossing the floor of the yard itself to pick up the building on the other side, making its way back out on to Cork Street and through the grotto archway to Brabazon Street, where it joins in urban continuity with the ubiquitous brick streetscape of the Liberties.

OPPOSITE
Hudsons at home.

+ Timberyard Social Housing

LIVING IN THE CITY

The project for this new housing scheme, comprising 47 dwellings and a community room, was generated by the construction of the Coombe By-Pass, a traffic relief road cut through the historic residential area known as the Liberties of Dublin. A backland site was opened up and the urban design requirement was for a new street frontage to heal the wounds caused by the road engineering operation. The design centres on a new public space on the site of a former timber yard, making a residential enclave with its own sense of place. The existing site was empty and derelict except for the presence of a small statue, where local people brought flowers and came to pray. We decided to keep the statue in the same place, built into a niche in a public passage through the new building. The statue is now known as "Our Lady of the Liberties".

The scheme works between the six-storey scale proposed by the city planners along the new Cork Street corridor and the much smaller scale of the existing terraced houses behind the site. The new buildings are built in brick, with hardwood windows and screens to terraces and roof gardens. The windows are offset from each other in the elevations to express the different scale and hierarchy of living rooms, kitchens and bathrooms contained within the residential accommodation, and to emphasise the continuity of the brick surface. The walls are modulated with recessed porches, double-height terraces and projecting bay windows to give a definite sense of depth and urban complexity to the building's edge and to provide an interface between the private world of the house and the local neighbourhood.

The scheme provides scale and identity in a difficult situation. It makes a piece of living city and reasserts some sort of architectural continuity at the frayed edge of the old city. The new buildings are connected back through lanes and courts to the historic character of the Liberties.

Space for Architecture

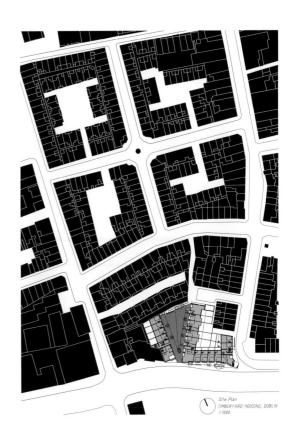

Site Plan
TIMBERYARD HOUSING, DUBLIN
1:1000

OPPOSITE
View from Timberyard
to the old distillery.

LEFT
City landscape skyline.

RIGHT
Site plan in context.

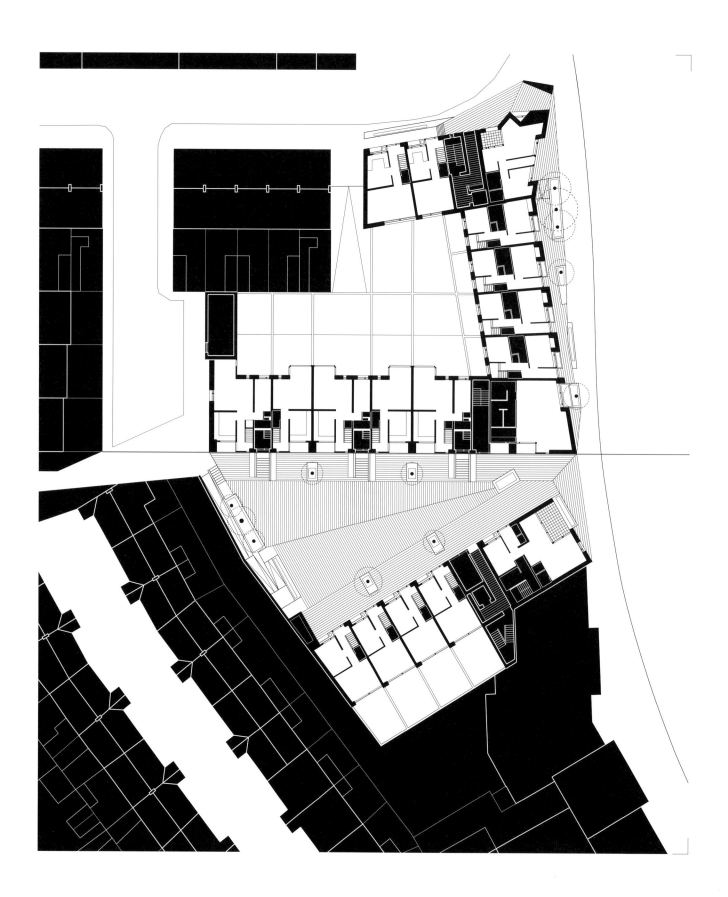

OPPOSITE
Plan, 1:450. Two-storey houses on the ground with duplex and single-storey apartments overhead.

RIGHT
Thickness and depth.

The World Outside

Space for Architecture

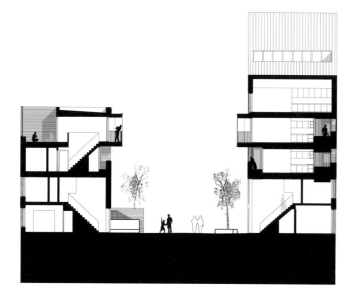

TOP AND MIDDLE
Study model, scale
1:100.

BOTTOM
Cross-section.

RIGHT AND OPPOSITE
Living in the city.

OVERLEAF
Urban scale.

scheme provides scale and identity in a difficult situation. It makes a
ce of living city and reasserts some sort of architectural continuity at
rayed edge of the old city.

London
Times

L ondon was the city of our second schooling in architecture, Sheila at the RCA, me at Stirling's office and later, on my departure for Dublin, she took my seat in the basement of 75 Gloucester Place. The second half of the 70s was a lively time to be a young architect in London. The AA under Alvin Boyarsky and Peter Cook's Artnet between them provided an architects' culture club, a continuous stimulus of lectures, exhibitions and discussion. We felt we had flown far from the confines of our Dublin background. The world was opening up. We began to see our Irish identity in wider terms, well connected to European traditions. There was an emphasis on the history of the European city. We became enthusiasts for European cinema. We followed the films of Herzog and Wenders, Resnais and

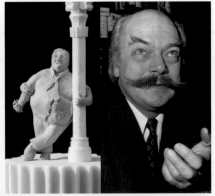
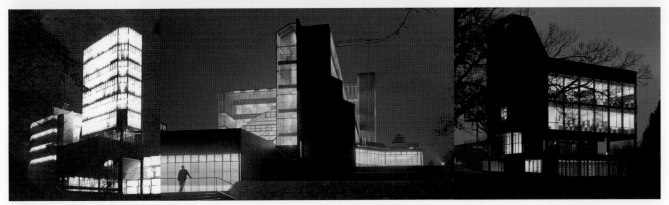

Rivette, Bunuel and Fellini, taking the underground to the Phoenix East Finchley, cycling to the Gate in Notting Hill and the Gate in the basement of Patrick Hodgkinson's Brunswick Centre, walking to the Academy in Oxford Street where they made their own posters for each new film. Late night movies were part of our daily routine.

We were reading Norberg Schulz's *Meaning in Western Architecture*, listening to Frampton's lectures at the RCA, struggling with Tafuri in translation and tracking a new way of thinking about cities through Rossi's recent writings. Studying in Dublin we had been wholly caught up with British architecture and English

OPPOSITE
London skyline.

TOP LEFT TO RIGHT
Queen's College, Stirling, 1971; Lyric Theatre competition design, 2003; Stirling, 50th birthday cake; Gaston Berlemont.

BOTTOM
Leicester, Stirling, 1963; Cambridge, Stirling, 1967; CRID building, UCD 2003.

Brutalism. Now living in London we found ourselves working in a world that wanted to extend its definitions of architecture beyond those boundaries. I was the only employee currently working in Stirling's office who had actually been to see the Leicester building. Stirling himself was much more interested in exploring German Neoclassicism than in revisiting his own earlier work. The Dortmunder Architekturausstellung 1977 exhibition catalogue was closely studied in an effort to replicate the pattern of Weinbrenner's weather-stained stonework. Stirling had been reluctant to recognise Constructivist sources of inspiration for his red-brick university compositions. Now he seemed to relish the knowing quotation, deliberately to court what had been assiduously denied, to invite readers of his work to share in the ironic game of reference and seek out connections between past works and current projects. Immersion in this image-laden world was like

living through a non-stop slideshow — a slide into confusion of mind created by reliance on cross-reference from which it took some time to fully recover. Architecture may be partially communicated through visual images but it is much better understood by the experience of actual buildings.

Now that the postmodern controversy has faded into a short-lived little phase in the history of styles, it is clear to see that the compositional principles of Leicester are close to and consistent with those of Stuttgart: the former piled up on top of its red-tiled podium, the latter scooped out of a similarly declared this time stone-clad datum. The engineering building, modelled on a ship, exaggerates its sub-podium ventilation via a very large funnel. The gallery, referring to the terraced hillsides of Palestrina, ventilates its basement through big stone blocks pretending

ABOVE
Photographers' Gallery, context model, scale 1:500.

to have been knocked out of the wall, lying scattered on the ground from which the ruins rise. The slimline ships' railings first used on Leicester were fattened up to meet German building regulations. Jim Stirling enjoyed a joke, but this joking was in deadly earnest. The lasting lesson we learned from Stirling was to stick to the point, to stay true to the propelling principles of a project, to see the bloody thing through. We left London to start out again in Dublin.

1971 was the year the Photographers' Gallery first opened in Soho, very near Covent Garden. I had worked for a while, in the summer of 1971, as a street sweeper in Covent Garden Market. Mountains of watermelons and other rotting fruit had to be shovelled up into a truck every morning. The rest of the day was more leisurely spent strolling with a broom and barrow around the market streets and stalls.

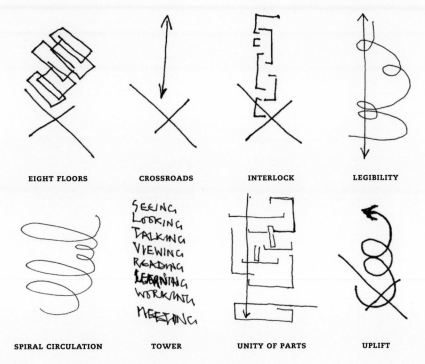

EIGHT FLOORS   **CROSSROADS**   **INTERLOCK**   **LEGIBILITY**

SPIRAL CIRCULATION   **TOWER**   **UNITY OF PARTS**   **UPLIFT**

WAYS OF SEEING

Hitchcock's *Frenzy* was filmed in the following year, set against the backdrop of this now lost London way of life. John Berger's *Ways of Seeing*, published that same year, was a key publication for our generation. His analysis offered a new way of looking at pictures, including photographic images. We spent many nights staring at the photographs on the walls of the French Pub in Dean Street, dreaming of Lilian Dredge on her racing bicycle, talking to Chicago the boxer and Ron the boiler-coverer and we once met the man who drew Biffo the Bear for the *Beano*. Gaston Berlemont, the patron who was born in the bar, was another avuncular influence in our London life. We had first gone to the French because we had heard that the Brutalists used to meet there to talk about architecture—no sign of them now—but still a wonderful place for discussion and drinking and to become our spiritual home for the time being.

ABOVE
Sketches, competition entry.

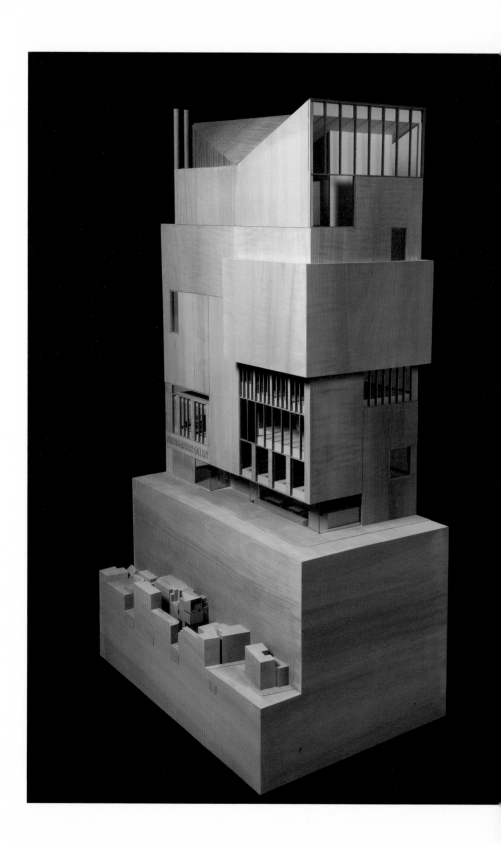

Space for Architecture

Memories of London times were evoked by the invitation to participate in a competition for a new building for the Photographers' Gallery, to be relocated to a new site, but still in Soho. 25 years after leaving London, never really having left it for very long, it was good to be asked to think about building in the centre of the city, the London we knew well. The rules of the competition were a little strange: no PowerPoint presentations, no design layouts and no models allowed. We tried to indicate our approach through simple diagrams, to articulate the restricted conditions of the site and to sketch out an architectural concept through a storyboard sequence that borrowed from Bob Dylan's "Don't Look Back".

Ramillies Street was half a level dropped down from Oxford Street. The site was at a narrow crossroads where some space could be carved out to create a meeting place. Space sacrificed at street level could be regained above to provide useful gallery dimensions overhanging the street corner. The eventual upwardly spiralling scheme was based on interlocking adjacencies between sunken café, mezzanine bookshop, education rooms and open galleries on upper floors and vertically skewered on a structural liftshaft. The mostly blind facade was to be finely dressed in Venetian red stucco lustro and glimpsed in corner perspective. The building form was derived from a chancy parable of a geological shift that might once have given rise to disruptions in the ground plane, as if a seismic shift had ruptured a crack in the continuous cliff wall of Oxford Street and at the same time caused sudden breaches in the building line of the new gallery. This small public gallery was to have been the first new Arts Council funded building to have been built in the centre of London since the 60s. Westminster city council planners appreciated the first principles reading of the context and the crafted detail of the design. The scheme was granted planning permission without delays, appeals or objections. However, Stirling's advice to architects setting up in practice—"expect to be building one in 12 that you design"—has proven to be not so pessimistic as first it sounded. Sorry to say, the fundraising target was reduced by the gallery board in the face of the financial crash of September 2008 rather than risk the loss of the funding at hand. We were naturally disappointed but we weren't sulking. It having been decided to convert the existing warehouse building, we worked with the gallery to turn that conversion into a more throughgoing transformation. But in fisherman's language, this is the story of the one that got away.

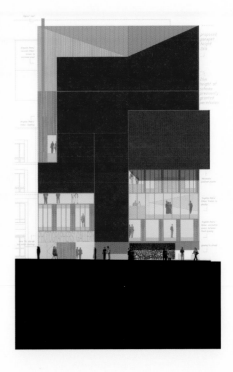

OPPOSITE
Photographers' Gallery, planning model, scale 1:100.

ABOVE
Elevation, planning permission, 2008.

+ The Photographers' Gallery

WAREHOUSE TRANSFORMATION

The Gallery is located at a crossroads, between Soho and Oxford Street. The corner site is visible in a glimpse view through a crack in the continuous shop frontage of Oxford Street. Ramillies Street is approached down a short fight of steps, leading to a quieter world behind the scenes of London life, a laneway with warehouses and backstage delivery doors.

The brick-faced steel-framed early twentieth century warehouse building is extended vertically in lightweight construction to minimise the increase in load on the existing structure and foundations. The extended volume houses large gallery spaces for changing exhibition conditions. A close control gallery is located within the fabric of the existing building.

The extension is clad in a rendered surface, a dark overcoat that steps forward from the face of the existing brickwork, like a close-fitting camera case. The street front café is finished with black polished terrazzo. Untreated hardwood timber framed elements are detailed to appear to slide into the wall thickness, flush with the rendered surface. The composition of hardwood screens and new openings combines with the existing to give a carefully crafted character to the transformed facade.

A deep cut in the ground floor facade was made to reveal the café interior to the street corner. The ground floor slab was cut out to make a wide terrazzo stair leading down to the basement bookshop. An east-facing picture window and the north-light periscope window were added to open up the interior to the London skyline.

A deep cut in the ground floor facade was made to reveal the café interior to the street corner. The ground floor slab was cut out to make a wide terrazzo stair leading down to the basement bookshop.

Space for Architecture

PREVIOUS PAGES
Café interior,
ground floor.

OPPOSITE
Inside outside.

RIGHT
View from Great
Marlborough Street
to Oxford Street.

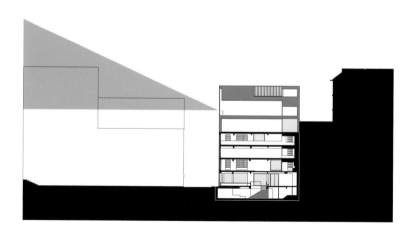

TOP
Top floor gallery.

BOTTOM
Section with view to
Oxford Street.

OPPOSITE
View to Oxford Street
from top floor gallery.

Space for Architecture

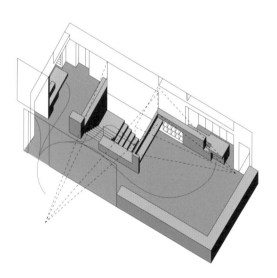

TOP
Nighthawks.

BOTTOM
Axonometric, ground
floor café, carved out
space.

OPPOSITE
Plan, scale 1:450. Top
floor gallery space.

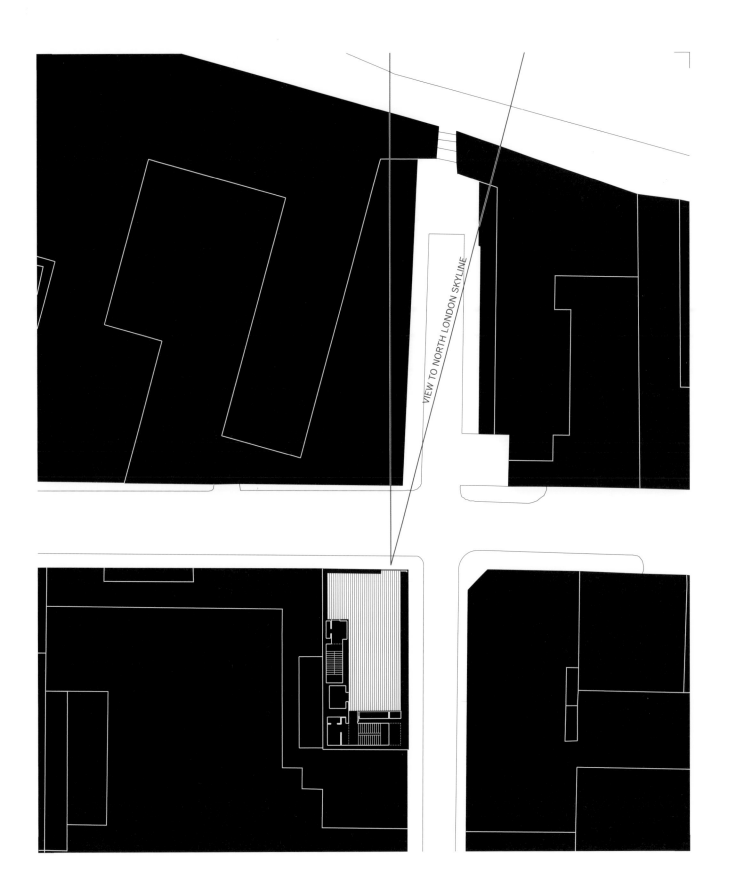

VIEW TO NORTH LONDON SKYLINE

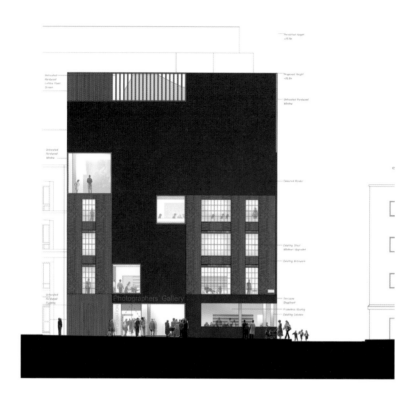

Space for Architecture

OPPOSITE TOP
East elevation.

OPPOSITE BOTTOM
North elevation.

RIGHT
View from Oxford Street.

Subtraction and Addition

W e've always worked with old buildings. This experience has profoundly affected how we work, to the extent that we don't really distinguish between projects for new buildings and re-workings. It's a matter of degree. All sites contain markers and contextual imperatives; we are always working in the context of existing conditions. These conditions are even more evident when a built structure is part of the site.

The story of our practice could be told through a series of relationships with existing buildings, each of which has influenced our way of working. Each experience has been remarkable in different, sometimes obscure, ways and the lessons we have learned have been distinct and cumulative.

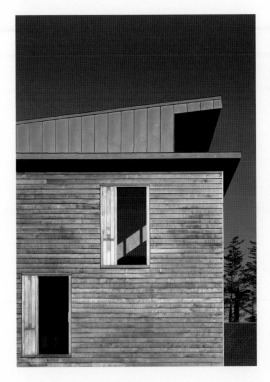 

When we came back from London to Dublin, we imagined that our role might be to build small-scale, socially useful civic buildings in Irish towns. As we left London a good friend had told us, half-jokingly, to "go back and change the face of Irish architecture", and, half-jokingly, we held onto this as an idealistic dream. We were inspired by the idea that architecture could have a role in defining a society, and we came back to find ourselves in a society undergoing cultural and social change. The Arts, especially Theatre, seemed to reflect the rapid developments occurring. Everything was in flux and it was possible, indeed necessary, to contribute to the discussion and to be part of the change.

By the end of our time in London we had become disenchanted with the lack of rigour in the ethos around us, architects plundering history for motifs and quotations,

OPPOSITE
Furniture College
Letterfrack, 2001, old
industrial school and
new workshops.

LEFT
Furniture College
Letterfrack, library.

RIGHT
Furniture College
Letterfrack, Connemara,
new and old.

hoping that this would give instant meaning and depth to their work. It all seemed to remain on the shallow surface. This excess did not connect with the empathy we felt for the deep economy of the ruins of the Palatine Hill and the farm-villas of the Veneto. We came back to Ireland and got back to basics.

We learned to drive a car so we could explore the landscape of Ireland. We looked at tower houses, castles, villas and monasteries, at earthworks, walls, barns and farmhouses. These different structures seemed to share an attitude to site; a direct starkness in how they met the ground, different from the English countryside, more defensive and much tougher.

We felt the same sense of discovery as in our early visits to Italy and Greece. As if we were seeing things which had been long forgotten or had disappeared from conscious memory; making connections between things previously considered to

be disconnected, or simply not considered by architects at all. We became aware, as we travelled the green countryside of Ireland, that we were traversing a constructed landscape. The natural takes on the guise of the man-made: a rock outcrop might be used as a retaining wall. Or the man-made uses the natural: tended ground employs natural ridges to define containment. Red corrugated barns, stone towers, ruins and whitewashed farm walls emanated potency and presence. Layered one over another in practical accretions, often in pleasing compositions, farmhouses had been built onto Mediaeval tower houses and single-storey sheds abutted national monuments.

This time it was Maurice Craig's books we carried with us. *Ireland Observed*, a slim gazetteer, concisely recorded many a remote ruin and drily elaborated on several oddities we thought we had discovered ourselves. In his *Classic Irish Houses of the Middle Size*, Craig argued for the innate classicism of Irish country houses, linking

Space for Architecture

the modest houses of gentlemen farmers with the Palladian mansions of Castletown and Russborough. We saw that the great Irish houses were closer in spirit to the working farms of their Italian origins than to the more refined character of villas in England. We had come full circle: visiting Palladio in the 1970s, with the barns and outbuildings integrated into the composition, we had been reminded of the Irish houses. Now the Irish houses brought us back again to Italy.

And there were so many ruins, neglected ruins, left in their natural state of decay, not managed or tidied up or rebuilt to fix them arbitrarily in some ideal moment in time. Ruination compresses time. Soft layers and fragile finishes, whose style might be used to date the building, these ephemera have disappeared, slowly stripped away by weather or aggression, and what survives are the utter walls, the terraced ground, essential enclosures that may have been indoor or might have been outdoor and could be 100 or 1,000 years old. Their value is not defined by their period. It's in

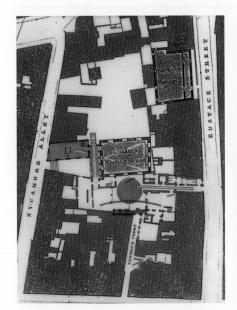 

their material form, how they meet the land. They are cultivation and construction. We could read them—and much more than one reading is possible when constructions from different periods have been overlaid. Material facts and known history make ruins appear to be immutable, but in reality they are more ambiguous. Walking around on the traces of old walls cut down to ground level is like moving through a plan drawing—it's possible to speculate on what the building might have been, or what it might become, because this contemplation of ruins is close to the sense of anticipation offered by building sites. Seen in this way, a ruin is like a building site; full of potential as much as laden with memory.

Contrary to our half-formed expectations, our first significant commission was not to be the design of a new post office on a corner site in some provincial town. Instead we were asked to work within a tightly compressed group of eighteenth

LEFT
Irish Film Centre plan, 1988, drawn over Ordnance Survey map 1847.

RIGHT
Site before refurbishment.

and nineteenth century buildings on a hidden site in central Dublin with no unbuilt ground and no significant street frontage. The project was to convert the former Quaker Headquarters into a centre for film and film culture. The site was at the centre of a city block with narrow threads of connection to three streets. An accumulation of nine buildings of varying age, quality and condition, the place had curious geometrical collisions and corners, an interesting history, an exciting cultural programme—and no immediate funding prospects. It was made for us. The initial concept, to uncover a central space, came quickly. To make it a reality tok a little time. This long slow project was to involve us in considerations of history and time, structure and material, dark and light, urbanism and typology, cinema and architecture.

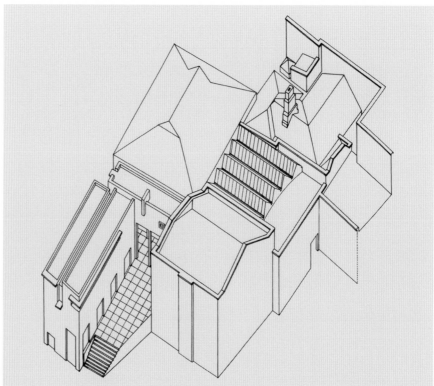

Measuring the dimensional, constructional and historical particularities of each of the nine structures clarified their individuality and, perhaps paradoxically, recording all this complexity allowed us to think of the collection of buildings as a single entity, which chance and accident had gathered together, a secret place in the city, in which we had been invited to act. We looked for the latent potential of this coexistent matter; tried to unearth the project lurking in this overcrowded terrain. By this process we arrived at a strategy of subtraction and addition.

Removing some parts clarified the relationship between others and reinstated their hierarchy, making more room for them to stand together. The addition of three

LEFT
Irish Film Centre,
Dublin, 1992.

RIGHT
Irish Film Centre,
axonometric.

new structures defined a route through and under the retained buildings, stepping and shifting between them, using compression and release to guide cinemagoers to the inside/outside foyer space at the centre of the Centre.

We don't work to fixed rules. We take each building on its own terms; immersion leads us to our conclusions. Immersion includes research, analysis and measurement, but it is not confined to these. It also admits observation and other less objective processes. We start with a number of fixed factors, the site and the brief — or place and use. The analysis of one is linked to the other. It is difficult to define the balance between the two. While measuring the dimensions of a building we are thinking about its future use and taking note of its character, atmosphere and textures. We relish the complexities involved in this activity: making a building in a particular place to house a specific activity. Doing this in the context of an existing structure with its own deep background and potentially conflicting conditions is an even more elaborate act. Sometimes one aspect takes on greater

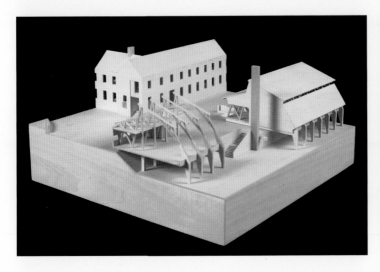

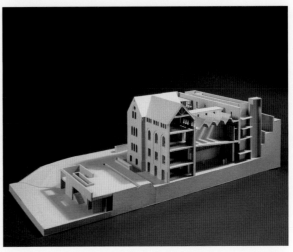

significance in influencing how we act; things loom out of obvious proportion, we don't always know why, but we go along hoping to find the architectural potential.

In hindsight, the final design can be described in a way that seems rational, or even sequential, but in truth, it is never really inevitable. The side-tracks, the distractions, the close-noticing distorted by our own tendencies, all contribute to the outcome and can be important generators of the work. This is one meaning of what Keats had called Negative Capability where "the poet receives impulses from a world that is full of mystery and doubt, which cannot be explained". Analysis is essential, everything must make sense, but this doesn't give you the form of the project.

An existing building is a present participant in the project, a character that has to be listened to, and this takes time because it doesn't tell you everything at once, or you can't understand it immediately. You are working on strategy and detail, on both from the very beginning. Material, light, texture, construction are part of the

LEFT
Letterfrack study model,
scale 1:200.

RIGHT
Good Shepherd Convent
University College Cork,
library/laundry, study
model, scale 1:100.

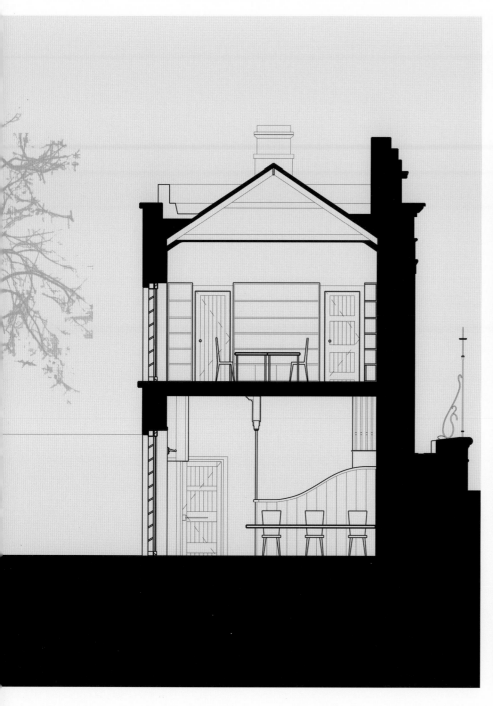

initial thinking; responding to existing buildings you are brought right up against the essentials of architecture.

In the late 1990s we were asked to rethink two nineteenth century religious buildings, both with harsh histories. The Letterfrack reform school and the Good Shepherd convent were repressive institutions that embodied aspects of their tragic past. Memories seemed to dwell in the surface materials and still to be carried in the spatial layouts. Both sets of buildings were simply axial and apparently obvious in the type pattern of their plans, yet somehow devious and confusing in the principles of their organisation. There was a toxic aspect to these buildings, and we felt they needed to be decontaminated. We had to think how to adjust and realign, to shift the axis and reinterpret the meaning, to separate the mere stuff of the structure from the tainted memory. We proposed strategic subtractions

to open up the interior to the outside air, and provided additional open spaces to clarify the closed in confusion of the past. Sadly for us to have to report, neither of these deeply engaging projects came to any kind of satisfactory completion.

Our own house is a kind of laboratory; an ongoing project that develops alongside us, that tracks the story of our lives. It is experiment and play. We try out ideas about construction, or space, or light, or old and new fabric combined. We use materials we have used in other projects, or test others for future projects. The left-over salvaged bricks from the Ranelagh School were used to make a floor in the garden. There have been three phases of work during 21 years of occupation. Each stage of the continuing project has had a different purpose and reflects a different frame of mind and another time of life. Each phase is engaged in conversation with office projects carried out at the time.

LEFT AND RIGHT
Architects' house,
garden.

Space for Architecture

The first phase of work, completed after we finished the IFI, revealed the structure of the house and established the strategy: how can a mid-nineteenth century three-storey house, built for people with servants, accommodate itself to our twenty-first century life? The second phase started after we finished the Glucksman and while we were working on the Lyric and the Seán O'Casey Centre.

Usually our understanding of the history of a building sets out guiding principles for the design approach. The facts and dates of its construction and the story of its progress, its uses and its users, from the beginning to our first encounter, are all shored up in each project. In the case of our own house the previous owner had erased most of the traces of occupation. To cram in the maximum number of bedsits he had blocked doorways and windows with showers. He had taken out stairs to the basement and built on a ramshackle set of extensions. The one

remaining original feature was a marble fireplace, which broke into fragments when he tried to rip it out, shortly after he sold us the house. His destructive actions created a *caesura* between the next move and the previous life of the house.

Our first works involved measured assessment, some subtraction and very little addition. Once extensions, cubicles and cheap linings were stripped away, we were left with the bones and lineaments of the house itself; the physical facts of its structure. Then we could see what we had. In looking at old buildings, there is often some element of surprise. In this case the chimneys, instead of being on the party wall as is normal in these Dublin houses, were built in the middle of the house, dividing the plan between hall and rooms. This meant that the usual arrangement of a front room spanning the full width of the house on the upper floor was not possible. We had to work with an arrangement of modest rooms, served and servant, on all

LEFT
Garden room.

RIGHT
Study.

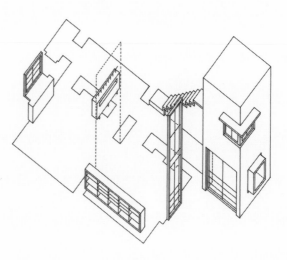

LEFT
Domestic details.

RIGHT
Initial intervention,
1992, axonometric.

Subtraction and Addition

floors. This constraining aberration of the type continues to intrigue us, and has influenced all three phases of our work.

The lowest floor, built as kitchen and servants' rooms, had low ceilings and was one metre below the level of the garden. The entrance floor, intended for formal family living, was disconnected from the garden. Wanting to connect living to garden we took out part of the middle floor to make one high room at the back of the house. We terraced the back garden in slow steps to bring the ground down to living level. These subtractive moves adjusted the hierarchy, establishing the former basement as the new living base of the house. The main rooms were connected by a 'studio section' into one complex space. A small wooden box with bathroom and study was added. A simple stair reconnected the levels to make it back into one house. Everything was light and bright; maple furniture and painted wooden doors. Heavy red oxide doors closed off the service rooms, grey-green glazed doors connected living rooms to the garden and the kitchen was Eileen Gray blue.

The second project, ten years later, comprised some additions to the house and further elaboration of the house-to-garden relationship. We added a new room at the back, using brick floors, granite-concrete elements and iroko structural beams, slats and windows: the materials of the Glucksman, the Seán O'Casey Centre and the Lyric Theatre. This garden-facing room fixed the high room like a Mediaeval hall at the centre of the house. It allowed parts of the house to be used in parallel by different generations coming and going, by-passing the open acoustic of the studio space. The library-bridge brought the materials of the garden room into the middle of the house. It entwined the second phase of work with the first. Outside, we consolidated the roughly scoped-out garden terraces in left-over brick, a staggered set of outdoor spaces extending from the new room. We also pushed back the ground from the front of the house, carving out a Greek-inspired small courtyard landscape, with steps and planting beds and a seat for sunny breakfasts.

The third phase of work started out as repairs and renovations, and, by a gradual series of small adjustments and surface linings, turned out to be a rediscovery of the potential of secondary spaces. An initially simple project to close gaps in shrunken floorboards led indirectly to the transformation of the front hall into a terracotta floored reading room. We worked in discussion with our builder and with the fabric of the house. We took advantage of the centrally-placed chimney to install a stove in the hall, on the 'wrong' side of the chimney. We re-used specially designed lights that had been rejected many years ago by the Film Centre clients as "too industrial". They seem quite at home in our house. After 20 years the new stair at last has its long-awaited handrail—a most complex project. The dimensions were tight. The brief was tricky; a balancing, supporting, protecting, shielding structure to be resolved in three dimensions. Handrails are hard. We worked again with the same good people who had made those troublesome lights. Together we treated this tiny tubular steel installation as an experiment, a carefully crafted prototype, perhaps for the next public project. And the next private project, someday, maybe, will be the studio at the bottom of the garden.

ABOVE
Bookshelves.

OPPOSITE LEFT
Double-height living room.

OPPOSITE RIGHT
Falling Dansu, 2012, writing bureau, collaboration with Joseph Walsh Studio.

+ Central European University Budapest

AN INTERCONNECTED CAMPUS

Budapest is a city of courtyards and passageways. The streetscape in this part of downtown Pest is repetitive in plot dimension and only slightly varied in parapet height, but many buildings are individualistic in expression. Balconies, ledges, bay windows and big cornices loom out over the building line, directly adjoining more restrained facades with regular windows. Most buildings date from the early nineteenth to mid-twentieth century. Each building has its own courtyard, usually located on the central axis of the plot.

The Central European University comprises five adjacent plots, between them taking up half of a city block. The land holding has frontages to three streets. The building plots are 25 metres wide and 50 to 60 metres deep. Adjacent buildings operate separately without interconnection. Party walls are the dominant feature, making a double thickness of separation from plot to plot. To move from a third floor classroom in Nador 11 to the same level in adjoining Nador 13, academic staff and students must go down into the street and back in again

next door. The courtyards are not working as an active part of the circulation system. The current campus feels like a labyrinth.

We proposed a phased strategy, making connections between existing courtyards, demolishing two inefficient buildings and designing two new buildings around a series of courts. All courtyards will be roofed over to provide a tempered environment from the climatic extremes in winter and summer. The courtyards are the campus, providing circulation system and social space. Openings are cut through party walls to provide visual connections between courtyards. Flying staircases connect department offices to teaching spaces. The project changes the relationship of the university to the city. Routes through the courts make new shortcuts through the city block. A new building on Nador Utca will provide a public face for the university in the city, on axis with the River Danube. The campus becomes integrated with the urban realm.

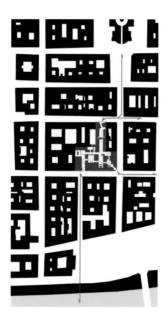

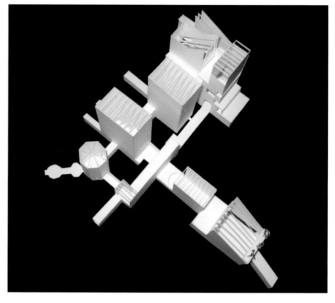

TOP LEFT
Nador 15 elevation,
scale 1:450, library
over learning café and
conference.

TOP RIGHT
Initial sketch, courtyards
connected.

BOTTTOM LEFT
The university in the city.

BOTTTOM RIGHT
Courtyard volumes
connected.

OPPOSITE
Plan, scale 1:450, phase 1
public entry and events
space.

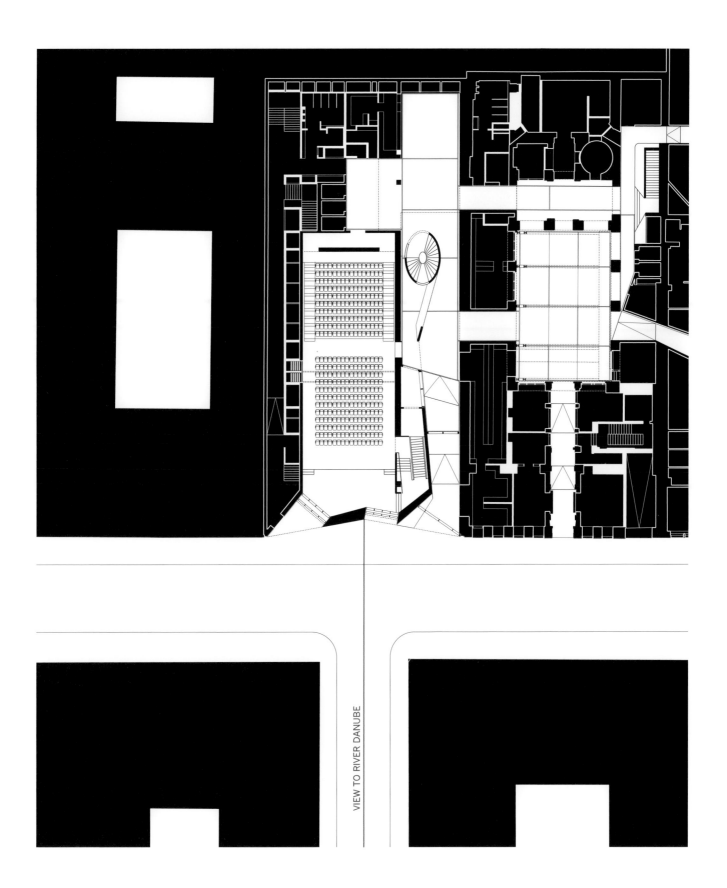

VIEW TO RIVER DANUBE

Subtraction and Addition

Venice
Excursions

In 1976, thinking ourselves finally finished with UCD, we set off together to see the villas of the Veneto. Sheppard and Jellicoe's *Italian Gardens of the Renaissance*, with its fold-out ink-wash sections of cascading terraces and dark lines of cypress trees, had been an inspiration to us as students. We arrived in Venice by train, staying only long enough to visit San Giorgio Maggiore and headed off to Vicenza to find Palladio. We stayed for a week in Hotel Diana on Piazza delle Erbe, our first floor window directly overlooking the Basilica. There was a pizza restaurant under the arcade where we ate every night facing the Loggia, served by a waiter who looked dangerous and very like Oliver Reed. We walked around the town to get to know the various palazzos and took a picnic lunch out to the Villa Rotonda. This was before the buildings were cleaned and forced by their facelifts to stand separated out from their ageless surroundings. We spent time studying the contested

Casa Cogollo, its surprising elevational similarities to Corb's early blind box house in La Chaux-de-Fonds and its evident comparisons to the stretched out section of the much later house in La Plata. Like most students of our generation, we had read Colin Rowe's *Mathematics of the Ideal Villa* and Wittkower's *Architectural Principles in the Age of Humanism*. We had the Dover edition of the *Four Books* with us, ready to note any changes to the ideal plans, marking up compromises in pencil on the margins. And we also had Akerman's paperback to hand, so we did not come to Palladio completely unprepared. Less expected was just how close and present these old buildings seemed and how open to interpretation and communicative of architectural intention. Palladio's plans were not locked up in the remote and historical past; each building was articulate of and specific to the particulars of its situation.

LEFT
Venice convergence, view to Filarete's column, February 2004.

RIGHT
Palazzo Barbaran da Porto, Palladio 1529, 1976.

Two years later we came back, this time on bicycles, to further explore the Venetian hinterland. The farmhouse villas, Saraceno unsymmetrically unfinished with its gates locked up, Poiana unoccupied but with its painted rooms open for us to eat our picnic, reminded us of the country houses in Ireland that owed their intellectual origins to the ideas built into these practical experiments.

John Berger has described history as the self-knowledge of the living mind.

> All history is contemporary history: not in the ordinary sense of the word, where contemporary history means the history of the comparatively recent past, but in the strict sense: the consciousness of one's own activity as one actively performs it. History is the self-knowledge of the living mind.
>
> JOHN BERGER, G.: A NOVEL

We began to see that we could read buildings, not as art-history of the passive past, but as surviving evidence of individual intention and collective intelligence, with

their inherent ideas alive in our time. This revelation emerged more as a gradual realisation, not as a sudden epiphany. Thinking back, regular visits to Venice across the past 40 years recur in our memory as sequential stages of awareness in this awakening process.

> It seemed to me that the theatre was in a place where architecture ended and the world of the imagination or even the irrational began.
>
> ALDO ROSSI, A SCIENTIFIC AUTOBIOGRAPHY

The Presence of the Past was the pedagogic title of Paolo Portoghesi's 1980 Biennale. From the top of the campanile we were witness to the tying up of the Teatro del Mondo at the tip of the Dogana. We watched Aldo Rossi step out of a water taxi onto the raft of what he called his "scientific teatrino", and later that night we saw him again sitting in the restaurant garden bower of Locanda Montin. We never met the great man himself, although we had learnt so much from his writings and his early work. Sheila has written about this in her introduction to the Blue Studio exhibition catalogue of 1983. Years later, our romance with Rossi came to a miserable end in the San Cataldo cemetery on a hot afternoon in Modena. Carelessly constructed, the realised building diminished the potential of this most beautiful project, the poetic complexity of its personal analogies reduced to a skeletal diagram, its melancholy stripped of mystery. That bad day in Modena marked the dead end of any affiliation with or lingering reliance on the Rationalist School of reductive typology. We said our goodbyes to the Tendenza and took the train back to Venice to begin again.

Another time, on a happier day, we took time off from our honeymoon in Venice, taking the train to join the Stuttgart site office party to celebrate the completion of Stirling's Staatsgalerie. I had worked on that scheme in the London office from competition to working drawings. Jim seemed taken aback to find his work so widely welcomed. "They all seem to like our new building" he murmured, "— we must be doing something wrong!"

Venice has no new buildings, not in our lifetimes, but its continuous urban form is made up of centuries of contiguous development, a constant accumulation of buildings adjoining each other in compatible neighbourly adjacency, each new addition contributing to the complex diversity of the evolving organism. All the private palaces have water gates onto one of 150 canals, accessible second by land and first water. All the churches and scuoli are entered from the common ground of terra firma; 118 islands are connected to each other by more than 400 bridges. It is the most unlikely city in the world, comparable only to itself and systematically organised according to its own internal logic. To a visiting architect, the city presents itself as a unique urban species whose inherent qualities can be appreciated over time and momentarily may even appear to clarify with close attention. We are intrigued by the flowing convergent pattern of its urban morphology, its curiously angled corners and convenient pockets of public space. In Scarpa's mosaic floor for Olivetti in Piazza San Marco, individual tiles appear to float away from each other, loosely bound together in a hazy

LEFT
Teatro del Mondo Aldo
Rossi, 1980.

RIGHT
Rio de L'Arsenal, 2012.

texture, not a rigid grid. Likewise, the jostled lines of the Venetian street network, with its narrow calli interrupted by little jogs and dogleg sidesteps at bridge connections, combine to generate a loosely tessellated continuity of unfolding space. We have sought out something of the characteristics of that sense of space in our buildings.

UCD was one of 40 schools of architecture invited to exhibit at the '91 Biennale, a not very competitive sort of inter-school competition called the Venice Prize. We selected current project work from 4th and 5th year studios, mostly drawings and very few models. The students made up a wheeled wooden box, skinned in sized canvas, to pull the show together. Some of those students carried on to become influential teachers and critical practitioners in the contemporary culture of Irish architecture: Hugh Campbell, Tom de Paor, Martin Henchion, John Parker, Margaret Stephenson, Dominic Stevens and Simon Walker. The Venice Prize was exhibited in the brick columned hall of the Corderie, where we had seen the Strada Nuovissima in 1980.

 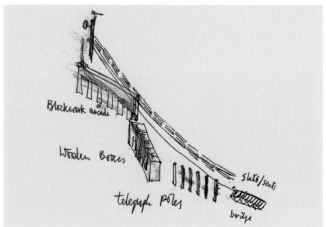

The '91 Biennale was the last time we met Jim Stirling. He had changed his habitual blue cotton shirt to green silk for the occasion of the opening of his Electra bookshop —to go with its patinated copper roof. The long boat-plan building was most carefully sited, moored between tall pine trees in the Giardini. He talked happily at a fancy lunch party in Harry's Dolci about his Irish friends, promising to come soon again to Dublin to visit the Film Centre, due for completion the following September. On 25th of June 1992, the day Stirling died, we were working on the competition design for Blackwood golf centre at Clandeboye. Our sketch design had some consciously intended similarities to his Leicester scheme, but turned over to lie on its side for landscape purposes. We finished the draw-up as some sort of sympathetic dedication or tribute to our mentor's design principles.

I believe that the shapes of a building should indicate—perhaps display—the usage and way of life of its occupants, and it is therefore likely to be rich and varied in its appearance, and its expression is unlikely to be simple. The collection

LEFT
UCD exhibition Venice Prize, Corderie, 1991.

RIGHT
Blackwood Golf Centre, competition design sketch, 1992.

(in a building) of forms and shapes which the everyday public can associate with and be familiar with—and identify with—seems to be essential. These forms may derive from staircases, windows, corridors, rooms, entrances, the total building could be thought of as an assemblage of everyday elements recognisable to a normal man and not only an architect.

James Stirling, AR, May 1975

We first came across Canaletto's *Capriccio Palladiano* published in Rossi's *Architecture of the City*. Canaletto assembled built and unbuilt designs by Palladio in a pictorial composition, an architectural fantasy presenting certain unrelated works in relation to each other and re-imagined in a Venetian setting. Rossi referred to this image as an illustration of his concept of the analogous city, an urban architecture formed

out of strangely familiar elements. The painting might also be seen to anticipate some of the speculative purposes of contemporary curators and commissioners of the Venice Biennale; an antecedent to the gathering of ideas, realities and imaginings from the world of architecture, to be set down beside each other in Venice, displaced as if in a dream.

Our most recent Venetian excursion was Vessel at the 2012 Biennale. Working diagonally across the way from the site of our students' show 21 years before, we once again chose to treat the historic structure as an active participant in the atmosphere of our exhibition. We wanted to invoke the material culture of boatbuilding and brick making, to assert the interactive potential of poetic intention and physical labour.

LEFT
Canaletto, *Capriccio con edifici palladiani*, 1742.

RIGHT
Vessel 2012, study model.

Space for Architecture

Vessel was a personal project, tracking our own preoccupations with contained and embodied space, but it was also a participatory project, involving artists and craftsmen, sculptors, writers and architects in a collaborative exchange. Its formal geometry was certainly closely related to the design development of the brick mountain pile under construction at the LSE. It might also have been wayside chapel, a contemplative shrine, a place apart from the noise of normal architectural practice.

Each of our installations at the Venice Biennale have explored aspirational aspects of real-life projects, removed at a distance from the boundary controls of their real-world actuality. Frustrated as we were by the half-finished campus for Connemara West, and somewhat depressed in the after-effects of the underachievement of so many worthwhile ambitions for the transformation of a badly blighted institution, especially in this arena which was so close to our heart, we used the Venice 2004 exhibition to re-express the intentions of the work in another way. We decided to tell the whole story again, in a different repetition, complete with all of its ingredients of culture and design, memory, matter and form. The complexities and contradictions of what most likely must now remain as a never to be completed work were amplified in resonance with the history-laden surroundings of the Arsenale. Mannix Flynn's memorable recital at the exhibition opening was acted out as a dance of symbolic rebirth, his dark suited figure moving in and out between the timber structures, his live performance playing off against the vital presence of the Open Frame and the Scary House.

When asked to make a film about the Cultúrlann Uí Chanáin building while it was under construction in Derry, to respond to the Irish group show curatorial theme of the Lives of Spaces, we made instead an animated doll's house, a "box of miracles" with snatches of sound and cycles of light, a son-et-lumiere inside a scale model of the as yet incomplete cultural space. The idea was to predict something of the future experience, a day in the life of a courtyard. How strange, sometime later that year at the opening event of the actual building, to find ourselves reminded of the merely simulated performance of our earlier installation. It was as if, for the new place to be understood in the deeper mind and accepted as something permanent, it had to be compared to a more fleeting image. The reassurance of déjà-vu made the real thing feel more like itself. Like walking in Venice, life sometimes takes you back on yourself and often seems to send you around in circles.

+ Transformation of an Institution

VENICE BIENNALE 2004

In response to the curatorial theme, "Metamorph", Ireland's Pavilion at the Venice Biennale was itself transformative of an unfinished project for the phased development of the former Industrial School and its eventual incorporation within a community generated campus at Letterfrack; the transformation of an institution.

The installation in the Arsenale was intended to tell the story of the past, present and projected future of the site. The exhibition focused in on the architecture of the new Furniture College and pulled out to provide an overview of the history, culture and landscape of Connemara West.

The new building at Letterfrack represents a rethinking of the relationship of the former penal institution with its place. Ireland's Pavilion recast elements of the architectural project to suggest characteristics of confinement and release, closed institutions and frameworks for change. Under the roof trusses of the abandoned Artiglierie munitions factory, separate structures confronted one another in an analogous composition. Principles of form and construction, abstracted from the built reality of a contemporary college, evoked memories of chapels and shrines, lobster pots and the skeletal carcasses of upturned boats.

An excerpt from the play *James X* was performed at the opening by the artist and author Gerard Mannix Flynn, himself a survivor of the Industrial School at Letterfrack.

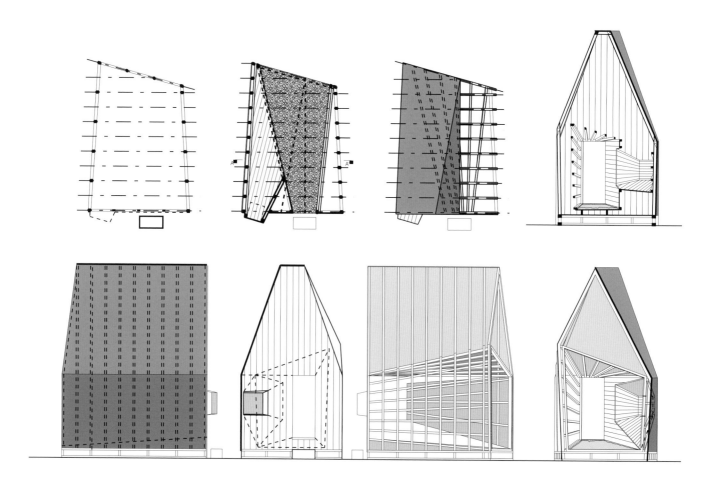

TOP
Scary House, design
drawings.

BOTTOM
Letterfrack, first sketch,
1995.

OPPOSITE TOP
Transformation of an
Institution, Venice
Biennale 2004.

OPPOSITE BOTTOM
Exhibition plan.

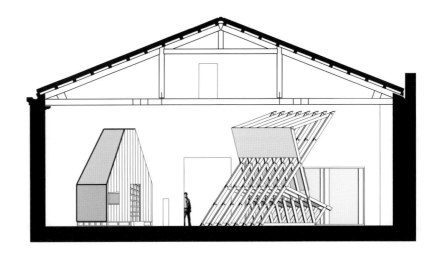

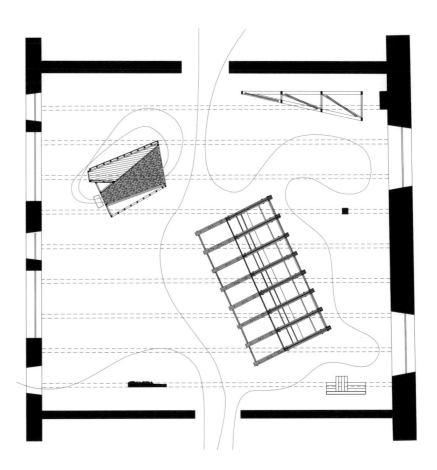

Space for Architecture

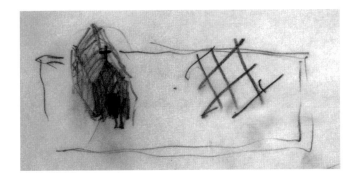

OPPOSITE
Transformation of an
Institution, Venice
Biennale 2004.

TOP
Scary House,
open frame.

BOTTOM LEFT
Concept sketch.

BOTTOM RIGHT
Open frame.

+ The Lives of Spaces

VENICE BIENNALE 2008

The installation focused on the social space of the Irish Language Cultural Centre. We wanted to revisit topics of investigation across our 20 years of partnership, beginning with the opening up of as-found structures to house the Irish Film Institute within the historic fabric of Temple Bar and continued through a series of private and public buildings, courtyard complexes and centrally organised plans. Refreshment and inspiration to continue our interest in the possibilities offered by the courtyard cluster typology had come from more recent visits to Japanese houses, Medieval towns, Moorish gardens and ancient Mediterranean settlements.

The armature contained a 1:15 scale model of the courtyard. Cuts through the external crust provided views into and across the central volume. A periscope, pocketed within the solid block, provided strange views down into the subtracted core. A light and sound installation animated the sensory experience of the physical model. Various two-directional viewing apertures revealed moving paths of light and shadow, to simulate the cycle of daylight-into-darkness in the space. Synchronised with the track of light was an acoustic composition incorporating sounds of human activity, speech and song—a day in the life of the building. Through this multi-media combination of cardboard modelmaking and microprocessor-controlled psycho-acoustic experience, we wanted to anticipate the real life of an as-yet uncompleted space.

COLLABORATORS
Lighting: Nicholas Ward
Sound: Jurgen Simpson

Space for Architecture

LEFT
Armature in Palazzo
Giustinian Lolin, Venice
Biennale 2008.

TOP
Courtyard model,
scale 1:15.

BOTTOM
View inside courtyard
as built.

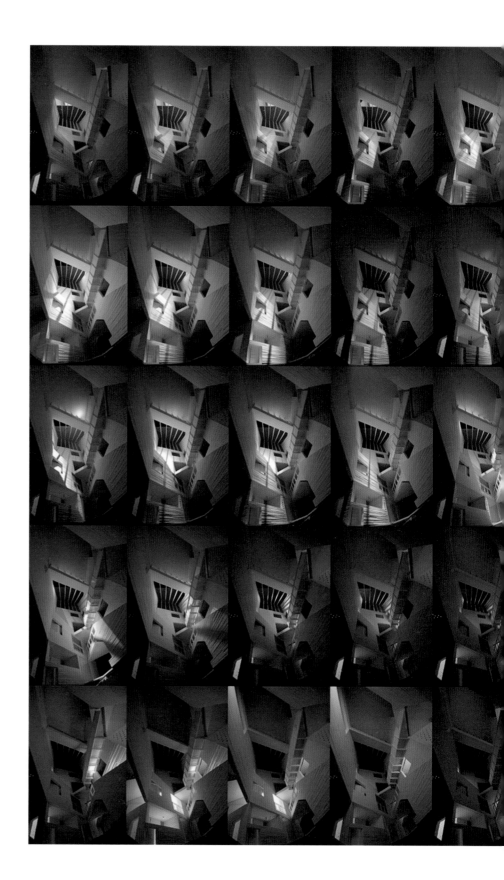

RIGHT
Up views of courtyard
model showing day to
night lighting.

OPPOSITE
'Within you without you.'

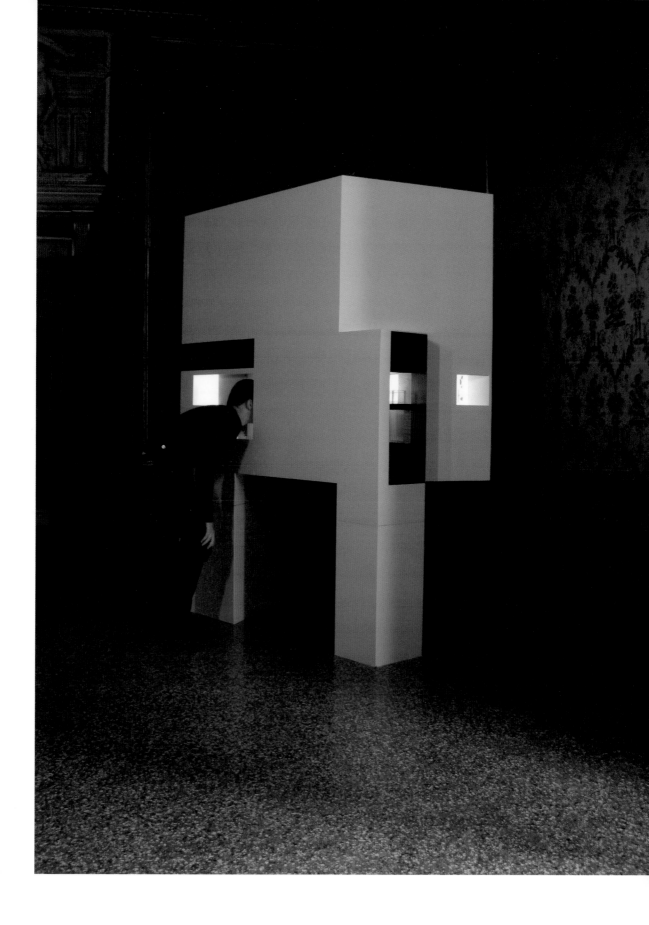

+ Vessel

VENICE BIENNALE 2012

The word vessel is suggestive of embodiment, enshrinement and containment. It carries associations with craft and circulation. Airship, boat, blood vessel, utensil.

Vessel was a site-specific response to the 2012 Biennale theme of "Common Ground", a plank-stacked timber structure in conversation with the layered brick construction of the Corderie. Vessel was a contemplative space hollowed out of solid matter, a light funnel, a lantern chamber, and a passage leading towards our common ground.

Literary and artistic affinities constitute our common ground. Architecture's deeper resonance is related to its wider culture. The work of other architects, artists, poets and performers sustains us. Their work provides inspiration for us to make our own work. Such affinities are part of our cultural context. We invoked precedent and invited practitioners to contribute to our installation. We remembered inspirational works and reflected on projects that run parallel to our own pursuits.

Bricks are cast from a mould, each special brick has to be hand-thrown from its own wooden casing. Clods of clay are dug out from the forest floor and the wood for the mould is cut from the trees. Brick and timber, the raw materials of archaic construction, have not changed much since the ship-builders built their vessels between the brick columns of the Arsenale.

CONTRIBUTORS
Dorothy Cross, Liam Flynn, Marie Foley, Seamus Heaney, Janet Mullarney, Tim Robinson, Peter Salter, Joseph Walsh Studio, Williams and Tsien.

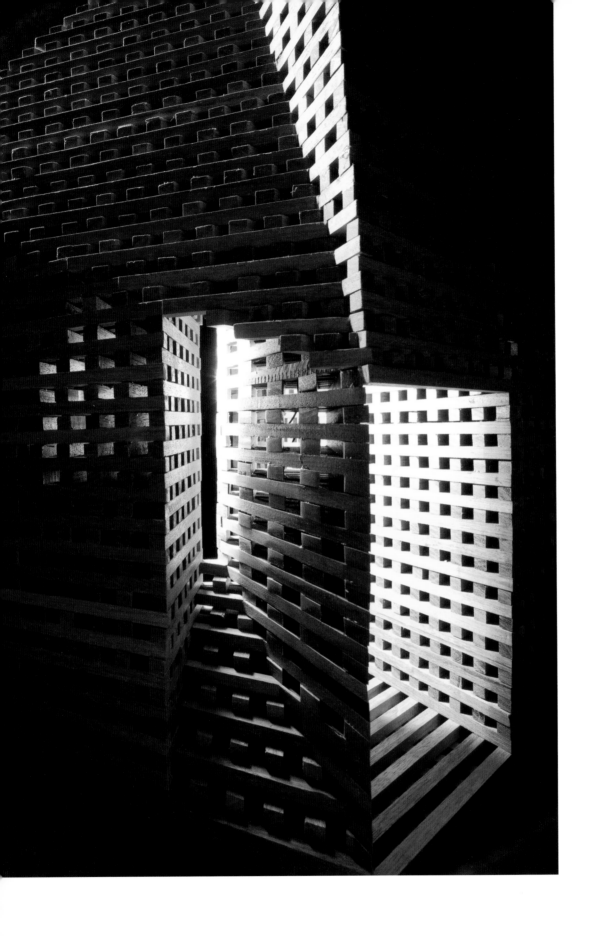

Space for Architecture

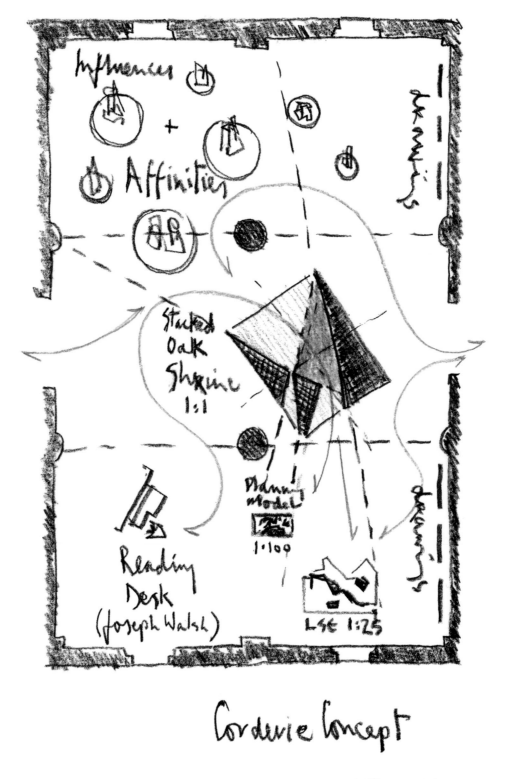

Influences + Affinities

drawings

Stacked Oak Shrine 1:1

Planning Model 1:100

LSE 1:25

Reading Desk (Joseph Walsh)

drawings

Corderie Concept

1:100

0   5

OPPOSITE
Model 1:10.

RIGHT
Initial concept sketch.

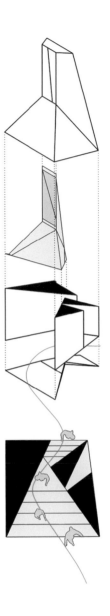

LEFT AND OPPOSITE
Vessel.

**OPPOSITE
BOTTOM LEFT**
Exhibition design
under construction.

**OPPOSITE
BOTTOM RIGHT**
Aldo Rossi, Monument
to the Resistance, 1962,
study model, scale 1:50.

Vessel was a contemplative space hollowed out of solid matter, a light funnel, a lantern chamber, and a passage leading towards our common ground.

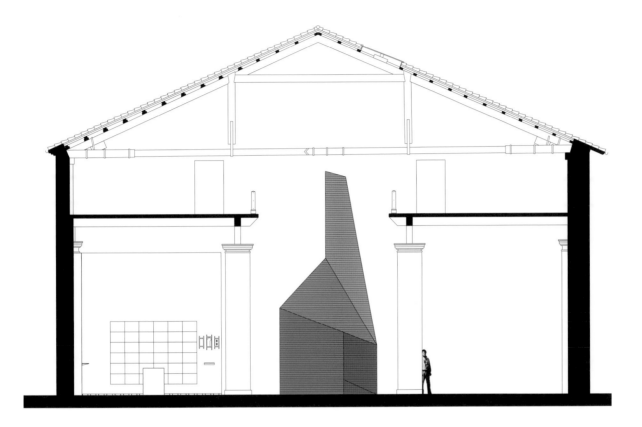

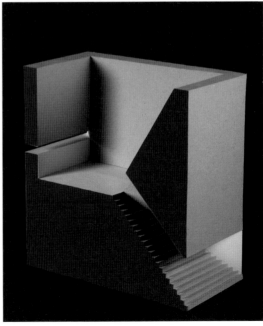

Space for Architecture

Venice Excursions

Building Ground

Extracting a project from the sense of the place itself is a kind of contradiction, as if you could divine a presence, an attitude, or an inclination by walking within a landscape, experiencing its orientation and weather, studying the characteristics of its culture; understanding the forces that act on it and have acted on it. We carry with us the sense of other places we have been, places that resonate with this one. But we are also inventing from scratch; using the stuff of the site to envision something new, not known or seen before.

Steps and platforms fascinate us. They elevate us above the surrounding world. Level changes, ledges and thresholds orchestrate how people move and pause. Stone pavements and grassy surfaces, the marks of man cut into a mountain, places made and enclosures established by cutting and filling the land to form a landscape where intent and purpose are ingrained, the dimensions of a step, the angle of its setting.

We have spent hours observing steps and seats outside the doors of archaic Greek chapels, the chapel itself sometimes half-swallowed by a rock face, noticing the singular quality of a small sacred space and how it is anchored to the Earth. Roof and walls make one continuous surface. Layers of whitewash unify the form. Low enclosing walls combine with seats and steps to act as skirting and plinth. The built ground is integrated with the building form.

Picking up a particular stone on the beach is not a casual or random activity; the eye is always sorting and sifting. While common criteria can't easily be defined, the precise selection method has become more certain over time. Stones with shared shapes are favoured, or those of common colour, but so are some erratic stones that fit in only by standing out. The most interesting stones seem to have been shaped by the forces of nature, their resultant form strongly defined. They

OPPOSITE
Watercoulour sketches.

LEFT TO RIGHT
Greek Island chapels.

are somehow complete, not to be added to or subtracted from. Shaley, friable fragments are not interesting. In this way a thesaurus of objects is compiled, including both synonyms and antonyms. The critical selection of a handful of stones can be compared to editing words in a phrase. They are turned over and scrutinized. Most are rejected. Drawing or painting the gathered stones means you take ownership of their form. It fixes them on a surface and in the mind. Collecting and grouping things in this way is part of the preparation for the eventual assembly of parts in a building, for the ordering and balancing of dimensions and densities, of heavy and light, of solid and ephemeral phenomena. The interest is not just in the physical characteristics of objects; it's in how the material qualities of things can influence deeper thoughts about life and use, relating to more profound and perhaps even metaphysical aspects of architecture, to how we experience things.

Sometimes things found in nature confirm something done by design.

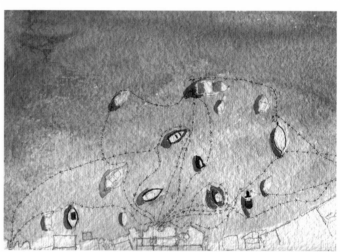

On the day that we heard we had won the LSE competition I picked up three angular terracotta coloured stones on a favourite beach in Greece, a beach full of smooth white rounded stones incised with dashed and dotted lines. Those LSE-specific stones jumped out of that familiar background—the gap between noticing and making suddenly diminished. Why do stones (and shells and wheelbarrows) matter? Because they are matter. They have their own material quality, they show the marks of time, altered by weather and affected by water. They embody characteristics of the place they come from. They are part of the ground we live on and build with.

Good maps are interesting because they describe the world factually. They convey the character of a place in quite a different way than photographs or drawings. Maps are made with a purpose. They edit places too, by focussing on some aspects and omitting others. They objectify our understanding of a place. The nineteenth century Ordnance Survey maps of Ireland describe topography and geology, land

and water, roads, and paths, bogs, geographic contours and rocks in layers of information. Field boundaries tell us about land ownership, land use and land quality. Words indicate place names and features, providing a complex description of a cultural moment. The map describes place and space in time. You can choose how much information to absorb; you can accept the bare facts or choose to go much deeper.

Maps and plans are part of our thought process. Drawing over the Nolli Plan, with each day's route through Rome shown in a different colour, I record our path as well as the fact that we do not choose to move through the same places in the same way each time. Our feet lead us, we mark that route on the map, and then the map itself suggests alternative routes: it leads us too. There are infinite ways of seeing and experiencing the city. We see something on the map that intrigues us and we search it out. The drawn-over map stakes out our Rome as a thing in itself, by acting on the map we claim the city.

Then there is the Venice map. Carefully colouring the water blue changed my reading of the city. It snapped from being an illegible labyrinth of routes and connections to a more comprehensible image of more than a hundred islands, each clearly separated by canals. The water defines the urban form; the bridges connect the island masses.

On holiday in a Greek island I swim into the harbour every day, lining myself up with a dark cave in the golden rocky headland opposite, then wheel around the blue boat to face the open sea, then aim for a peak on a distant hazy mountain range before turning to head back towards the ladder. I mark the route I've taken on the map I'm making. It changes with each swim; boats are added, moved or removed. The swims develop in response to the map. I see myself suspended in aquatic space between the many fishing boats. As I move I feel their shape and size because I have drawn them onto the blue-green watercolour sea. I adjust my route to check if that boat has really moved since yesterday, or if it's in alignment with that mountain monastery, or if the wind is coming up.

Space for Architecture

This swimming map unites objects and space. The elements are not fixed in place. It maps the space between things that are not quite static. So the space is not static either. It is liquid. Space is both that which separates things, defining and measuring the gaps between objects, and a thing in itself. It allows us to observe objects while it can also be perceived as a thing. Space shifts between positive and negative, between concrete and abstract. Describing the process of making his maps of Connemara, Tim Robinson says:

> While walking the land I am the pen on the paper, while drawing this map my pen is myself walking the land. The purpose of this identification was to short-circuit the polarities of objectivity and subjectivity, and help me keep faith with reality.
>
> TIM ROBINSON, CONNEMARA, HARVEST FILMS DIRECTOR, PAT COLLINS

Plans have always been the starting point for our work. Perhaps our plans have become more complex, but maybe they are also getting simpler and more intuitive.

They are less clearly driven by axes and compositional devices, of course those devices are there but they are less evident. They are more about movement, direction and balance. Plans are maps. They chart experience, culture and occupation. They anticipate the future rather than describing the present and the past. The act of marking maps, following our feet, fixes certain spatial conditions in the mind. That's why we strive to bring our life experience into our studio work—because what we are doing is building a world, or trying to project a new place in the old world.

OPPOSITE
Memory Box for
Williams + Tsien
Wunderkammer.

LEFT AND RIGHT
Mountains and chapels.

+ Howth House

LOOKING AT THE SEA

The clients had been living next door in a Victorian villa, a house of many rooms; they wanted a convivial living space that more loosely accommodated contemporary family life. Looking out to sea, with the sun on our backs, we discussed our shared preference for facing north, watching the effect of the light on the landscape, without the glare of the sun in your eyes — the quiet of standing in the shadow and looking at the light. Half way up the hill of Howth, overlooking the harbour, the site lies sandwiched between houses, blinkered by its boundaries and mesmerised by the outline of the island of Ireland's Eye.

A straightforward three-part plan and sectional organisation grew out of the site conditions. It was a condition of planning permission that the new house should not overlook adjoining properties or protrude beyond existing building lines. The house was designed from the inside out, or from the sense of being within the site looking out, and each development in the form was designed from first principles. A long wall is aligned between two trees which fix diagonally opposite corners of the plot, the body of the house turns to focus on the island, the walls bend to cup the space that flows between them.

These photographs of the lived-in house were taken 12 years after the builders (and the architects) moved out and the client moved in. The architecture of the house is enhanced by use.

LEFT
Family room.

OPPOSITE TOP
Inside outside.

OPPOSITE BOTTOM LEFT
Initial sketch.

OPPOSITE BOTTOM RIGHT
Outside inside.

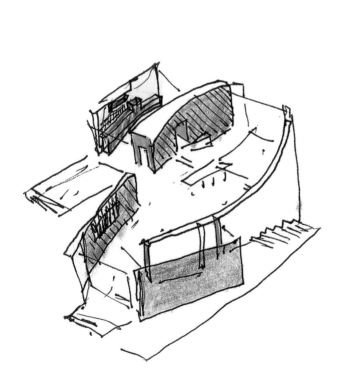

Building Ground

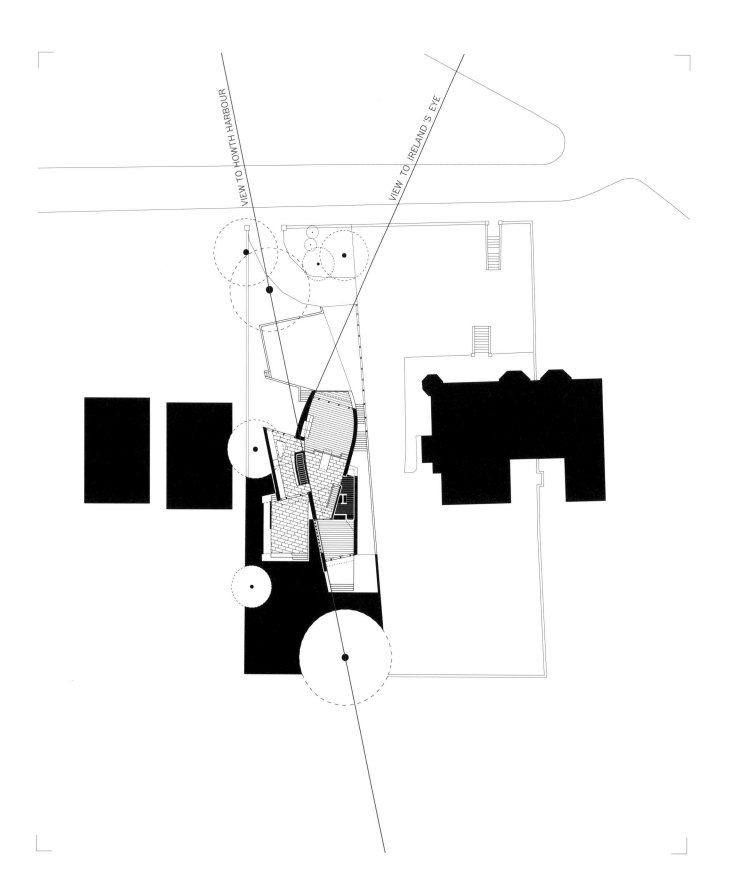

VIEW TO HOWTH HARBOUR

VIEW TO IRELAND'S EYE

Space for Architecture

OPPOSITE
Plan, scale 1:450.

RIGHT
View from the road.

Family room,
sunken terrace.

Space for Architecture

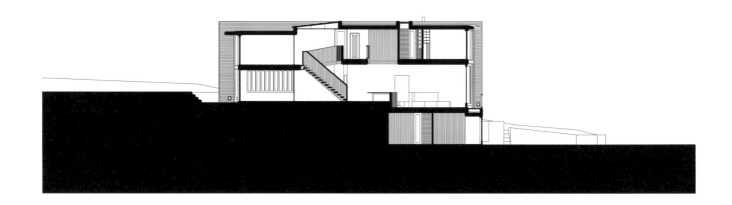

Half way up the hill of Howth, overlooking the harbour, the site lies sandwiched between houses, blinkered by its boundaries and mesmerised by the outline of the island of Ireland's Eye.

Space for Architecture

+ Lewis Glucksman Gallery
University College Cork

TURNING IN THE AIR

The Glucksman provides a cultural and artistic centre on the University campus, a civic space linking the college to the wider community. The building includes display spaces, lecture facilities, a riverside café and gallery bookshop. The building occupies a minimal footprint between mature trees which previously encircled two disused tennis courts. By building tall, at the height of the trees, the bulk of the building was reduced and the parkland setting of the University was conserved.

The podium is the point of access up to the gallery and down to the café. The entrance hall opens onto the Podium which intersects with the route of pedestrian approach from the main avenue and the riverside walk. The limestone podium relates the new building to the architectural language of the campus. It emerges from the limestone escarpment like a man-made extension of the natural landscape. Acting as a pier between the avenue and the river, it is both landscape and building, plinth and pathway.

The gallery is raised among the trees in an interlocking suite of rooms with selected views up and down the river, into the trees and towards the campus. The wooden vessel resonates with its woodland site. Gallery spaces are interconnected in plan and section to provide a variety of scale and lighting conditions appropriate to the exhibition of a wide range of art works and artefacts. At the core of the gallery sequence is a suite of close-control environmentally conditioned spaces, for museum standard display conditions and multi-media and acoustic performance.

The café opens towards the west into the parkland between the river and the limestone escarpment, providing views from the lower ground to the Neogothic quadrangle of the College above.

Space for Architecture

LEFT
The café is carved out of
the limestone podium...

OPPOSITE
... and the gallery is
raised among the trees.

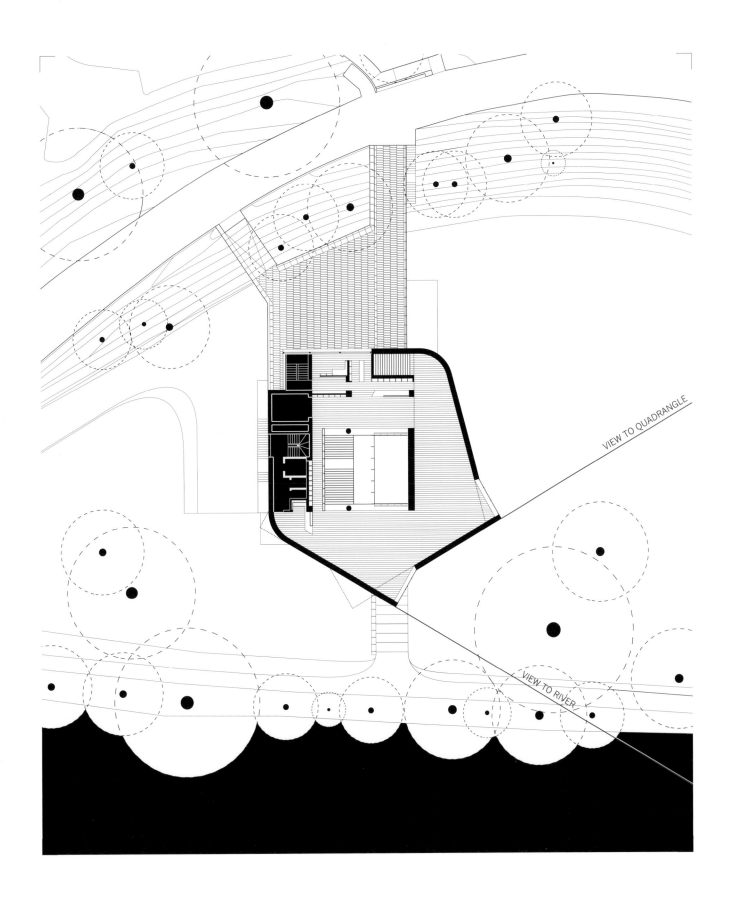

VIEW TO QUADRANGLE

VIEW TO RIVER

Building Ground   153

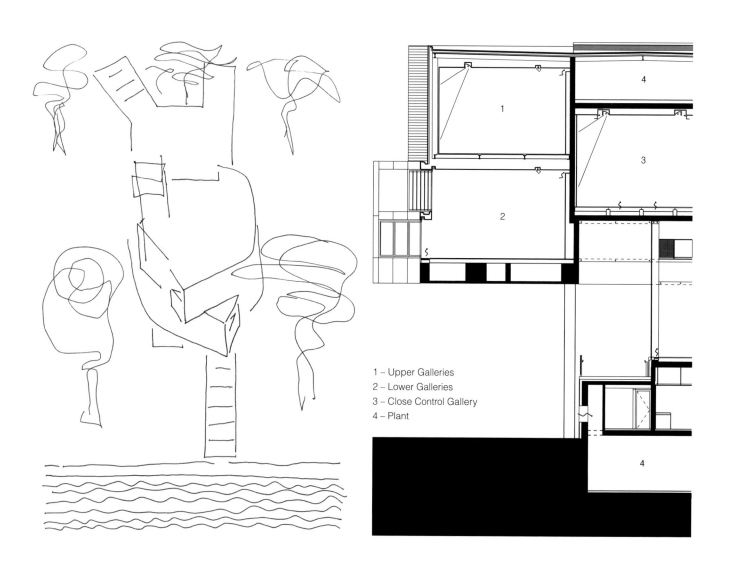

1 – Upper Galleries
2 – Lower Galleries
3 – Close Control Gallery
4 – Plant

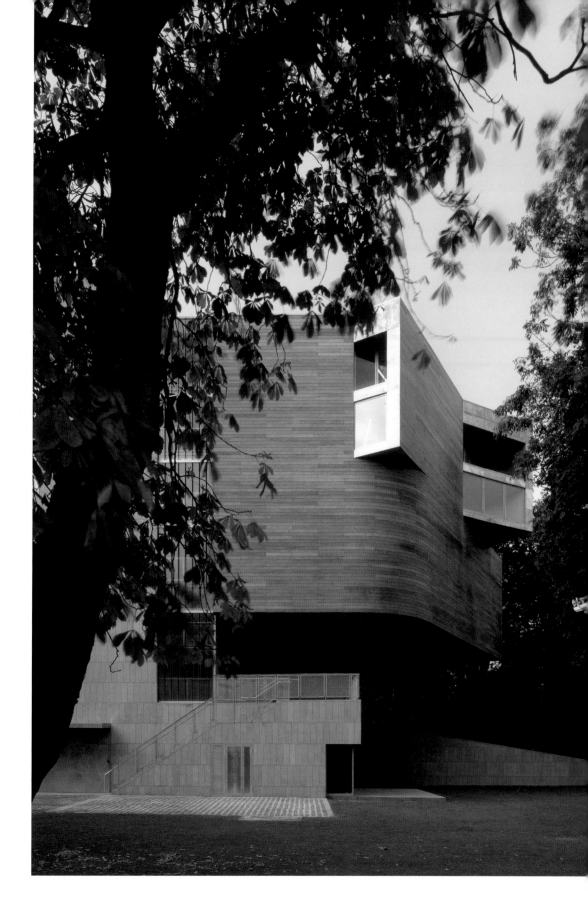

OPPOSITE LEFT
Design sketch.

OPPOSITE RIGHT
Detail section.

RIGHT
East elevation.

OVERLEAF
Upper bay windows.

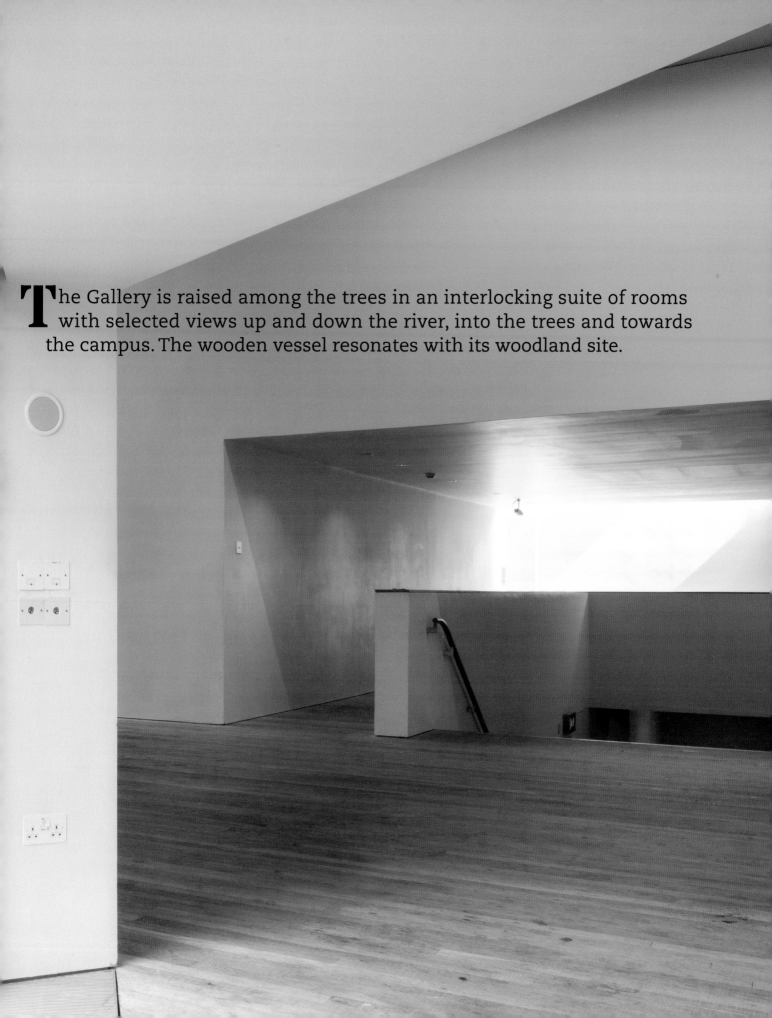

The Gallery is raised among the trees in an interlocking suite of rooms with selected views up and down the river, into the trees and towards the campus. The wooden vessel resonates with its woodland site.

Space for Architecture

OPPOSITE
View to the city.

ABOVE
View to the park.

Building Ground

Space for Architecture

LEFT
Public route under
inverted courtyard.

RIGHT
Undercroft.

Cat's Cradles

A good deal of our practice and much of our teaching activity has been caught up with the question of place. Another nearby patch of the declared territory of our enquiry is the careful plan, the operational mechanism of an efficiently functioning scheme, the craftsman's aspiration for an everyday working world of useful beauty. A little further beyond the social realms of place and the pleasures of purpose-made plans, and always allowing for practical interests in structure, material and public space, reasonable respectable values that would be shared by most of our professional colleagues, we might also have to admit to some more personal preoccupations, such as colour or character or form, or even with what one critic recently referred to as "tortured geometry".

Auden warned his fellow poets against risking the loss of civic engagement if they were too inwardly absorbed in the complexity of their own "cat's cradles". But what kind of poetry could be produced without inwardness? Inscape is a useful conceptual

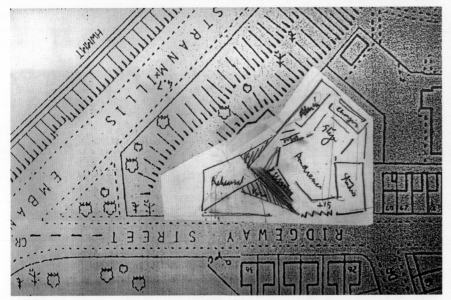

term that we might borrow from Gerard Manley Hopkins in this regard. And all good work has some sense of mystery in its making. Behind every architect's plan, underpinning what Palladio understood to be "the harmonious arrangement of parts", there lies the ordering exactitude of geometry. Sometimes the grid is explicit; a method of measure that regulates the placement of unitised partitions and made to fit prefabricated equipment. However, rectilinear grids are not always as utilitarian as they might seem. Le Corbusier's so-called Modulor made sense to nobody except himself, not even to his own studio. Paul Robbrecht has developed his own office system of prime-derived dimensional coordination, simply to avoid an unquestioning reliance on simple numbers. If there is a mystic spirit underlying Mies' house planning, any such sense of transcendence probably comes more from Katsura than cold science. The intellectual logic of gridded structures owes as much to Greek stereometrics as to rational engineering.

OPPOSITE
LSE Student Centre,
regulating lines.

LEFT
Lyric competition
sketch.

RIGHT
Irish Language Cultural
Institute under
construction.

This is to admit that there is a private side to architecture, a personal aspect internal to this most public of the arts. The elements of architecture, columns, walls, doors and windows, are the solid facts of physical building, but these elements also live in the mind. And they play on the minds of architects. Words can mean many differently unrelated things until connected together in context. Like complex words that make sense only when combined into sentences, the fundamentals of the language of architecture float free, abstracted and ambiguous, until they are applied to paper and put to work in a plan. A columned hall, a winding stair, a dark passage or a corner window seat are not neutral ingredients of a recipe, neither do they come readymade for any and every architectural design. Cooked up in the brain and played out on the page, such fragmentary phrases must be thoroughly tested for spatial composition and rhythmic volume before they are ready to be tried in the real world.

Snatches of space and special design tactics developed for one particular project can resurface in subsequent schemes. The Glucksman Gallery found its form by following the lines of force on its site, turning in the air to catch views in different

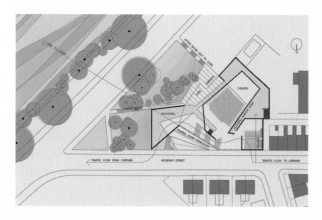
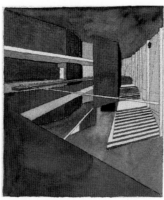
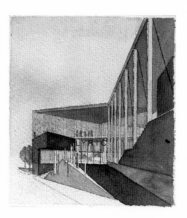

directions and in between the trees. The Lyric site, simply analysed, was too small to allow the building to be planned on one level and, to add to the difficulty, it was sloping steeply downhill. Joining the extremities of the irregular boundary into a diagram of intersecting lines was one way of dramatising the complexity of the challenge. Triangulating the site seemed to enliven the necessary task of arranging preset shapes of stage, studio and rehearsal. The Lyric was the first in a family of angled geometry schemes, a search for simplicity through complication that continues through to the LSE.

The regulating lines of the Lyric plan reach out to reconcile the rigid baseline of Ridgeway Street with the Lagan river's meander. The project is based on circulation flowing between opposing conditions, working a diagonal way across the plan between street grid and serpentine riverside. The angled geometry of An Gaeláras is intended to spring a public building free from the restrictions of a long narrow plot, restrained as it is on three sides by blind party walls. The central space is stretched towards the street and the facade is sucked in from the building

LEFT
Lyric competition, site plan.

MIDDLE
Lyric competition, foyer interior.

RIGHT
Lyric competition, entry forecourt.

line. These distortions are deliberate, disturbances calculated to encourage pedestrian traffic to divert from the life of the street, to engage with the cultural activities of the institution. A zigzag grid joins fixed column points that are evenly distributed along the party walls. The structure of the building is integrated with the geometry of the plan. The effect is to intensify the intuitive experience of the building. The pinball geometry orients all the elements of reception desk, café counter, stairs and circulation spaces in an orchestrated sequence, connecting all parts together in a courtyard cluster.

The house in Killiney, designed at the same time as An Gaeláras, is somewhat differently organised. Here the response was specific to a sprawling and three-

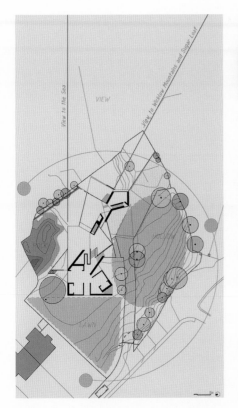

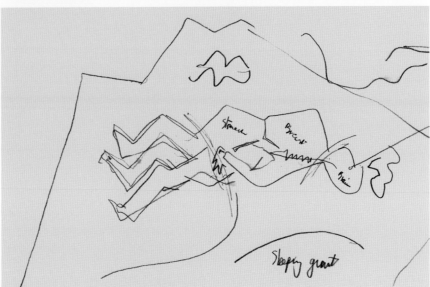

dimensionally complex site; there was the distant view to the sea, the immediate presence of a granite rocky outcrop, a sheltered central valley lying six metres below the road, and a relatively flat lawn with some well established specimen trees. Rilke once described Rodin's sculptural work as being centred outside itself, developing a feeling of spatial relationship between the viewer and the object viewed, rather than simply seeing the figure standing impassively isolated. He describes this space-disturbing effect as the result of vectors from the outside world working their way inwards to awaken the form into a vital presence, a living form in active engagement with its surroundings.

LEFT
Killiney House, site plan.

TOP RIGHT
Form sketch.

BOTTOM RIGHT
Sleeping Giant, concept sketch.

Space for Architecture

LEFT
Stepped landscape interior.

OPPOSITE TOP
View from the road.

OPPOSITE BOTTOM
Garden view, entrance elevation.

Cat's Cradles

Sometimes small projects can act like pilot fish for larger public works. Seen in this way, the dugout section of the Hudson House directly relates to the Ranelagh School, the sightlines of the Howth House seem to swim alongside those of the Glucksman, and the lineaments of the Killiney House might be seen as further experiments preparatory to the design of the LSE. The plan of the house in Killiney cuts back to register the presence of the rock, it wraps around the sunken valley garden and extends itself out to say hello to the sea. The section is stepped in half-levels to sit down low on the site contour. A canted concrete roof canopy hangs heavily over the plan, making the interior part cave, part tent. Overlapping spaces are pinned together by the central pivot point of a concrete chimney shaft that doubles as a light well.

Our search is not for the abstracted perfection of an ideal form, rather the reverse, designs are derived from careful studies of site constraints, by a process of close-noticing of local conditions. The idea is to arrive at a resultant form that speaks back to and makes new sense out of its existing situation, to approach a deeper sort of simplicity through acceptance of the complicated origins that make up the shape of things.

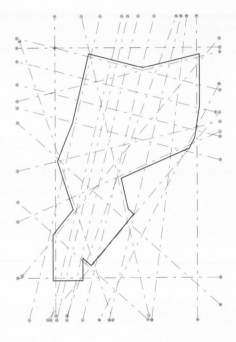

An elaborate network of laylines was developed to set out the plan and section of the LSE Students' Centre. There were requirements in the competition brief for upper storey setbacks to comply with rights to light. Parapet heights were to be determined from planning restrictions. The brief was to house the many and varied activities of a students' centre at the intersection of an open street campus. Responding to these demanding constraints from first principles allowed the building to lean a little away from the established street line, to stand somewhat separate from its given boundaries, to create a canopied social space on the street instead of the expected internal atrium. Each facet of the design relates to particular circumstances and a site specific geometry controls the facetted form. By a process of objective analysis and subjective response the object is made subject to its setting.

Alberti began his treatise *On the Art of Building* by defining a building as "a form of body". He believed that buildings consist of "lineaments and matter, the one the product of Thought, the other of Nature". According to Alberti, lineaments form the building's rational organisation, let's call that design. Matter, in Alberti's sense of the word, comprises the bones, muscles and skin of the animal body, the raw material of architecture. We might think of our creative work as oscillating between two conditions, between lineaments and matter, between design and raw material, between inwardness and the outside world, between the poetic and the practical aspects of an open-minded investigation. In this sense, very little has changed in the secret life since Alberti first made his claim for the autonomy of architecture as an intellectual discipline.

OPPOSITE
LSE competition, street life concept.

ABOVE
LSE underlying gridlines.

+ Irish Language Cultural Centre

CULTÚRLANN UÍ CHANÁIN

An Gaeláras is designed for public life and community involvement. Its inwardness is not an anti-social reaction or a defensive strategy forced by any client requirement or retreat from society. The intention is to enhance the appropriation of collective space by locating the focus of the architectural project within the organism of the building, to find home territory embodied inside the experience of the structure rather than expressed through exterior representation.

The landlocked site is contained on three sides with one narrow end facing the street. A continuous terrazzo floor connects the footpath to the building interior, minimising the barrier between outside and in. Activites are clustered around an internal court that provides a heart to the body of the building at the confluence of its circulatory systems.

The scheme starts from the central court, which is thought of as an outside room, an empty tower house locked within the form. A glass-roofed board-marked concrete trapezoidal courtyard is carved through the four floors of the building, with steel stairs, bridges and platforms crossing and overlooking the skylit volume. Each floor level is associated with one of the functions of the Irish language institute: culture, enterprise, teaching, and administration.

The nature of the site prevented any light or view from three party walls. Light spills into the central court through the inverted rooflight. The different functions of each floorplate are made legible by the complex overlapping geometries of the structure.

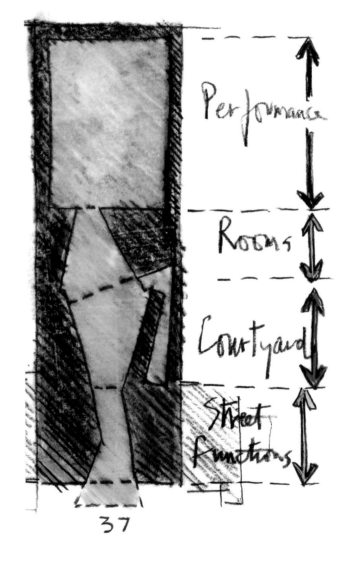

37

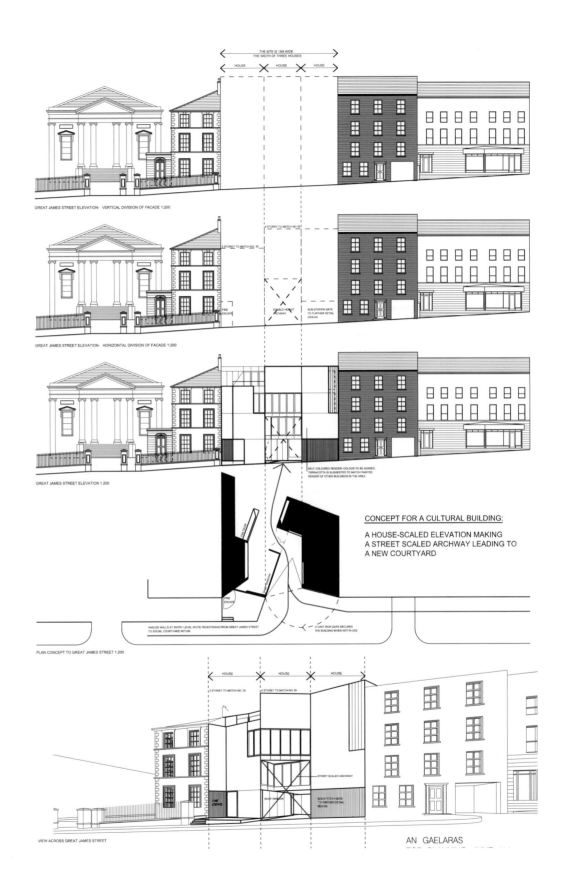

GREAT JAMES STREET ELEVATION- VERTICAL DIVISION OF FACADE 1:200

GREAT JAMES STREET ELEVATION- HORIZONTAL DIVISION OF FACADE 1:200

GREAT JAMES STREET ELEVATION 1:200

CONCEPT FOR A CULTURAL BUILDING:

A HOUSE-SCALED ELEVATION MAKING
A STREET SCALED ARCHWAY LEADING TO
A NEW COURTYARD

PLAN CONCEPT TO GREAT JAMES STREET 1:200

VIEW ACROSS GREAT JAMES STREET

AN GAELARAS

OPPOSITE LEFT
Great James Street.

OPPOSITE RIGHT
Concept sketch.

RIGHT
Elevation analysis at
planning permission.

OVERLEAF
Extended courtyard
space.

Space for Architecture

Cat's Cradles   175

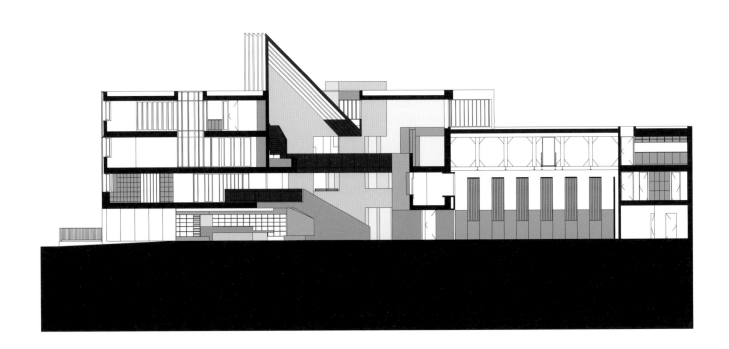

Space for Architecture

**OPPOSITE TOP
LEFT AND RIGHT**
Hume-Adams talks,
opening night.

OPPOSITE BOTTOM
Long section.

RIGHT
Vertical circulation
made visible.

Cat's Cradles

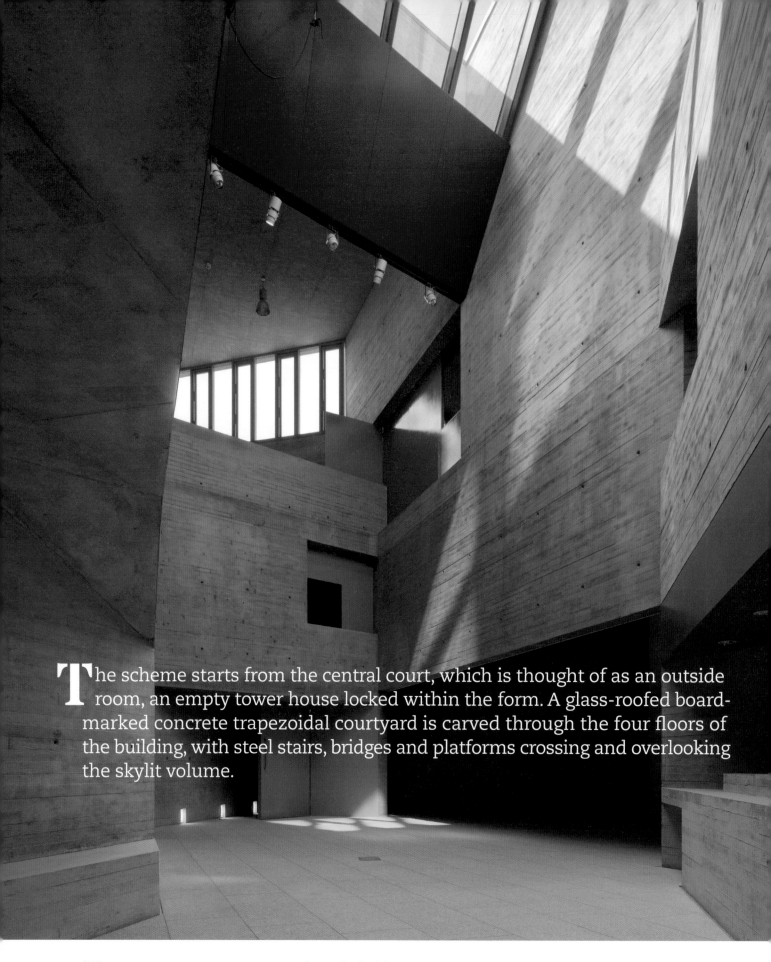

The scheme starts from the central court, which is thought of as an outside room, an empty tower house locked within the form. A glass-roofed board-marked concrete trapezoidal courtyard is carved through the four floors of the building, with steel stairs, bridges and platforms crossing and overlooking the skylit volume.

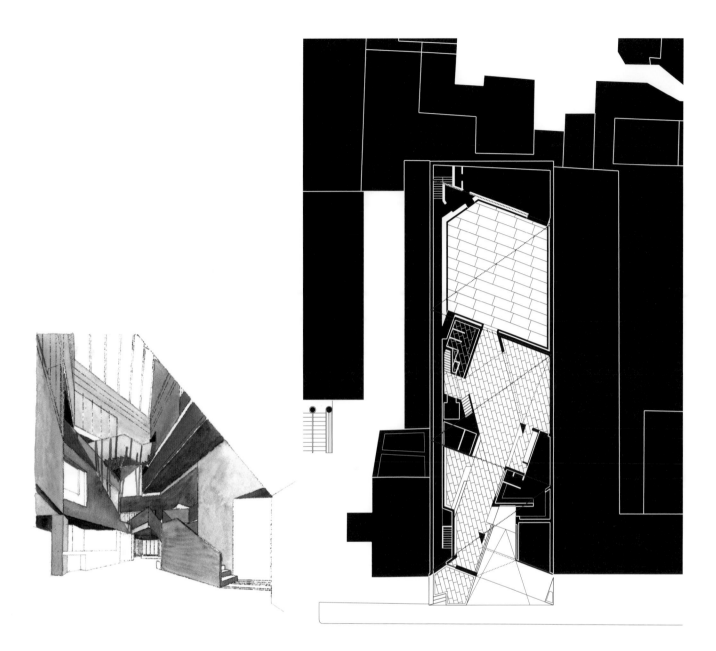

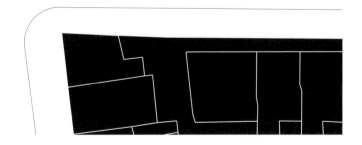

OPPOSITE
Daylight in
the courtyard.

LEFT
Daylight study.

RIGHT
Plan, scale 1:450,
performance space,
foyer, café, information
desk and street-facing
gift shop.

Cat's Cradles   179

+ The Lyric Theatre

A HOUSE FOR LYRIC

The Lyric Theatre stands on a sloping site at a triangular junction between the grid pattern of Belfast's brick streetscape and the serpentine parkland of the River Lagan. The building site was tightly restricted and irregular in shape. The budget was strictly limited. All the building materials were selected to endure and crafted to weather with age.

The skyline displays the principal elements of a producing theatre, mainly solid volumes closed to view. Transparent social spaces flow around the fixed forms of auditorium, studio and rehearsal. Three acoustically isolated brick boxes stand in the circulatory system like rocks in a stream. There are three different points of entry, one for trucks and two for people, all tied to existing street levels.

The auditorium is a single parabolic rake, running counter to the slope of the site, with services in the undercroft. The spatial scheme maximises sightlines and generates intimacy, with the feeling that the actors are in the same room as the audience. The seating layout is creased along a line between two entrance lobbies. The timber floor folds slightly in plan and section, like an open hand, to hold the body of the audience together, focused on the stage and within sight of each other. The facetted timber lining is tailored to accommodate the sometimes conflicting requirements of stage-lighting, sightlines and audience acoustics.

The studio is a six meter high brick-lined "empty space". A picture window with a sliding shutter allows for occasional visual communication between street and theatre activities.

The rehearsal room dimensions are related to the main stage and studio. The acoustics of this room allow for recital and readings. The new building replaces a substandard structure built in the 1960s. The building is the result of an open architectural competition held in May 2003, and eight years immersion in the complex process of briefing, design, fund-raising, demolition and construction.

Space for Architecture

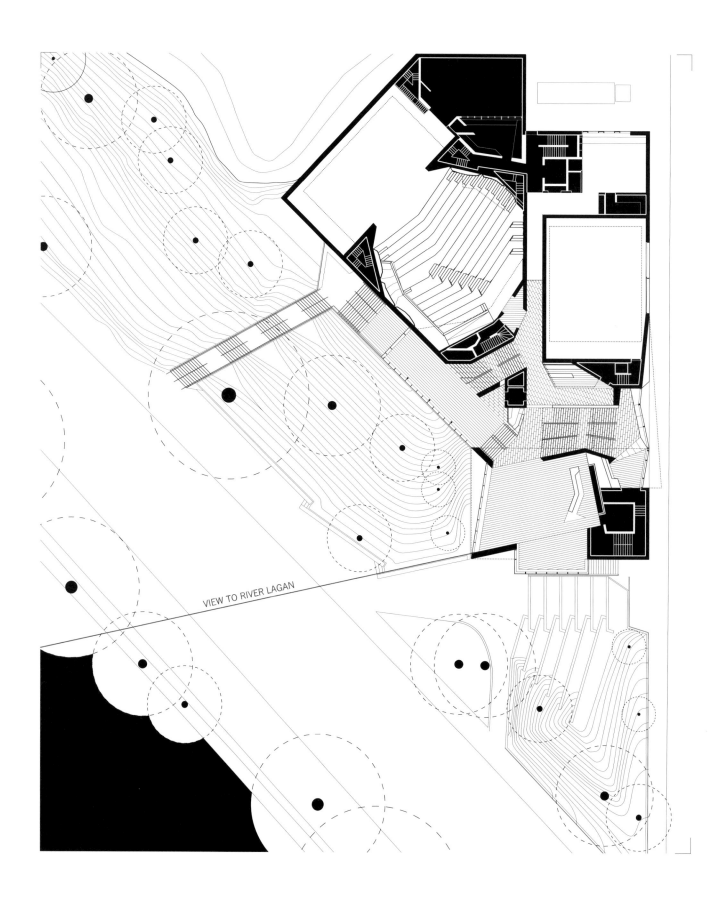

VIEW TO RIVER LAGAN

OPPOSITE
Plan, scale 1:450,
auditorium for 400,
studio for 150, bar and
rehearsal room above
the bar.

ABOVE
Lyric woods.

ABOVE
The Lyric woods and
outdoor auditorium.

OPPOSITE TOP
River elevation.

OPPOSITE BOTTOM
Planning model.

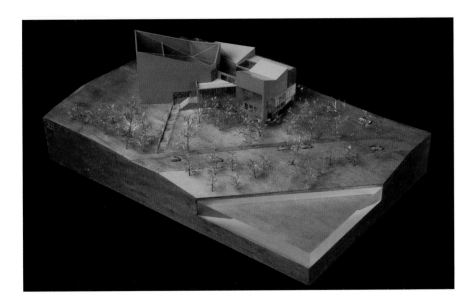

Cat's Cradles 189

Space for Architecture

Transparent social spaces flow around the fixed forms of auditorium, studio and rehearsal. Three acoustically isolated brick boxes stand in the circulatory system like rocks in a stream. There are three different points of entry, one for trucks and two for people, all tied to existing street levels.

PREVIOUS PAGES
Brick floors, hardwood
screens, concrete
ceilings, Jean Prouvé
furniture, lighting
constellations, flowing
social space.

ABOVE
The long hall...

OPPOSITE
... overlooks the River
Lagan.

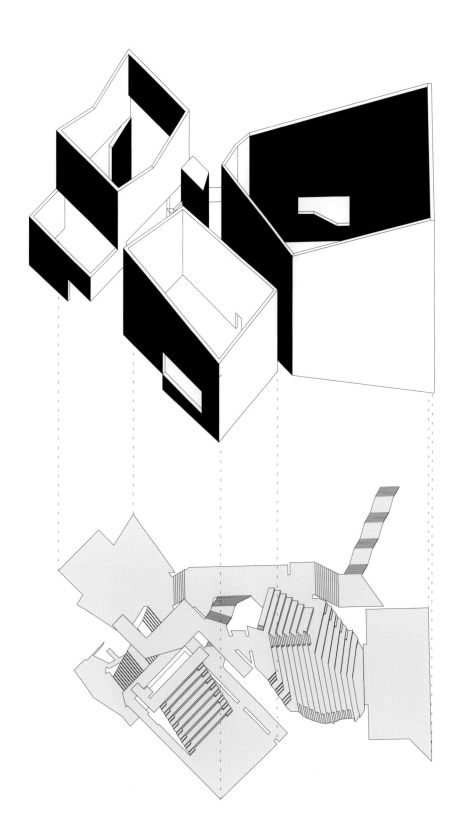

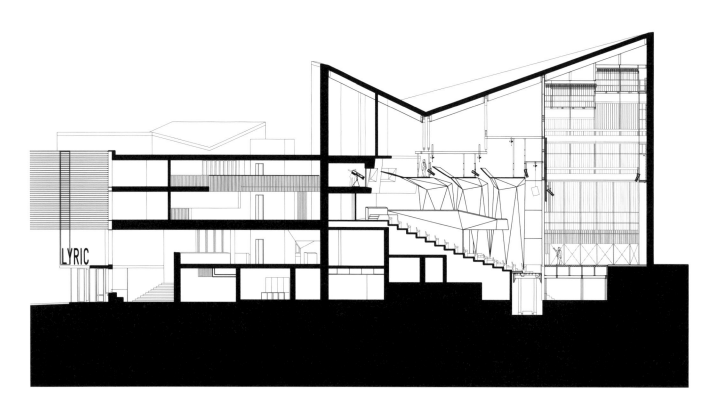

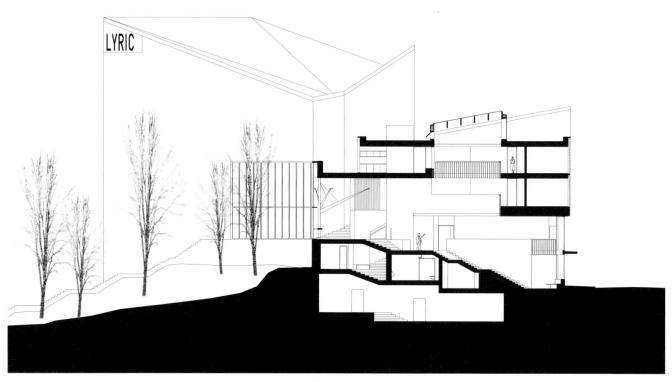

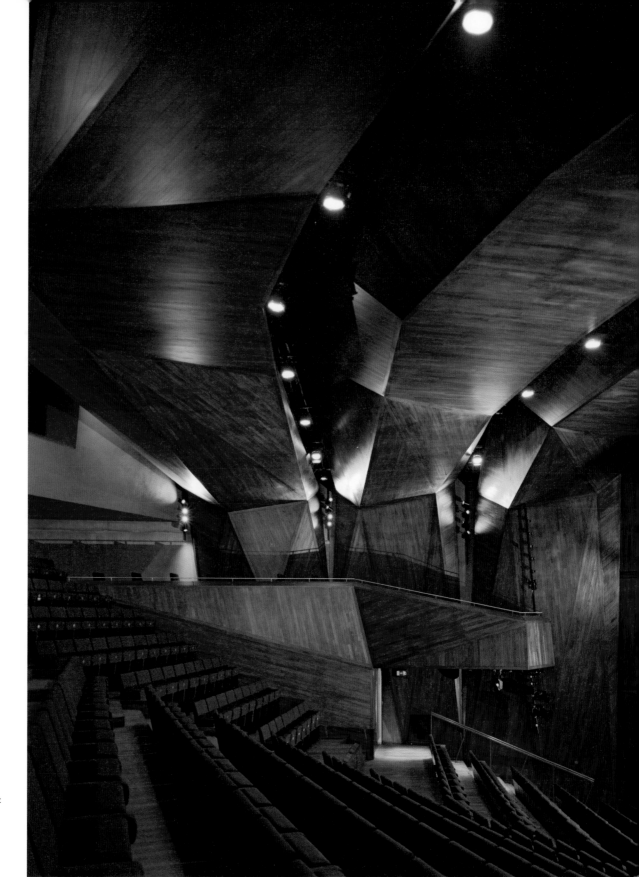

Cat's Cradles   197

+ Saw Swee Hock Student Centre London School of Economics

STREET LIFE

The site is located at the knuckle-point convergence of narrow streets that characterise the London School of Economics city centre campus. The folded, chamfered, canted and faceted facade operates with respect to the Rights of Light Envelope and was tailored in response to specific lines of sight along approaching vistas, designed to be viewed from street corner perspectives and to make visual connections between internal and external circulation. The surface of the brick skin was cut out along fold lines to form large areas of glazing, framing views from street to room. Like a Japanese puzzle, the design was assembled to make one coherent volume from a complex set of component parts. Analysis of the context influenced the first principles of the design approach.

The building embodies the dynamic character of a Student Union. The complex geometries of the site provided a starting point for a lively arrangement of irregular floor plates, each particular to its function and each working into the next by an intricate system of spatial configuration. Space flows freely in horizontal plan and vertical section, with stairs twisting and turning to create diagonal break-out spaces throughout the building.

London is a city of bricks. The building is clad with handmade paving bricks, used in a new way, with each brick offset from the next in an open work pattern, wrapping the walls in a permeable blanket, creating dappled daylight inside and glowing like a lattice lantern at night.

The building has the robust adaptability-in-use of a lived-in warehouse, with solid wooden floors underfoot. Steel trusses or ribbed concrete slabs span the big spaces. Circular steel columns prop office floors between the large span volumes and punctuate the open floor plan of the café. Concrete ceilings contribute thermal mass with acoustic clouds suspended to soften the sound. Every landing has a bench or built-in couch. Every hallway has daylight. There are no closed-in corridors.

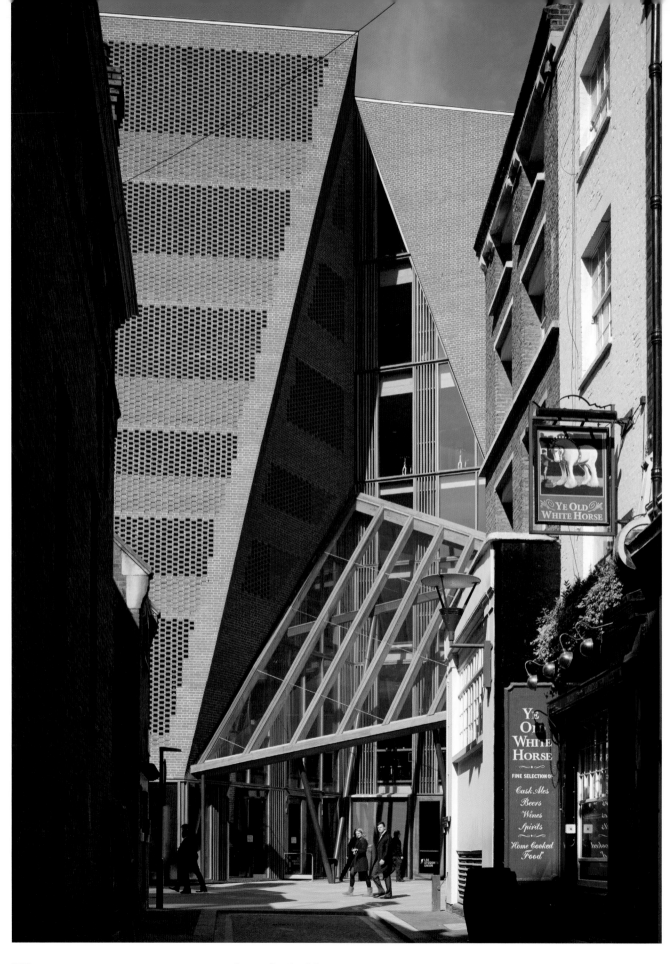

Space for Architecture

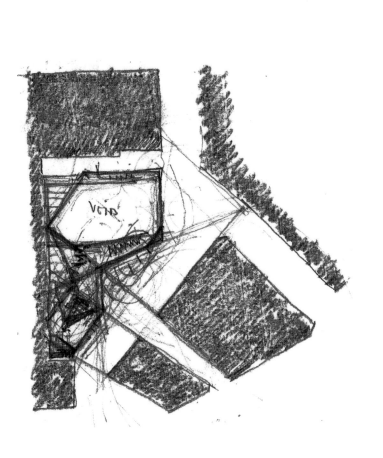

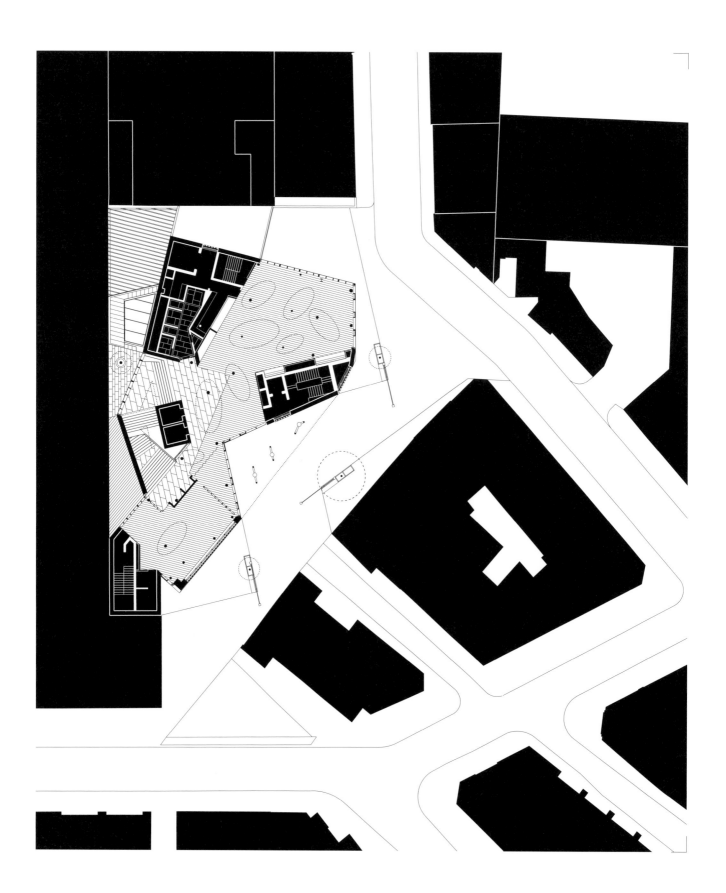

Space for Architecture

OPPOSITE
First floor plan, scale
1:450, learning café,
kitchen servery, toilets
and student activity
space.

TOP
Building in context.

BOTTOM
Planning model.

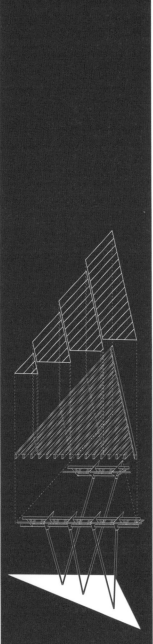

Space for Architecture

LEFT
Entry forecourt,
glazed canopy.

TOP
Entrance canopy detail
design study.

OPPOSITE
Competition elevation
design.

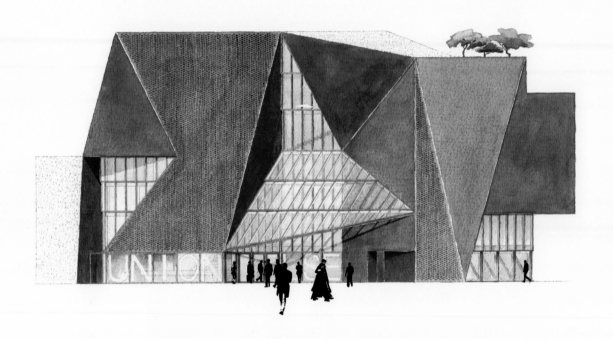

Space for Architecture

LEFT
Uplift.

OPPOSITE
First floor arrival to
learning café.

Space for Architecture

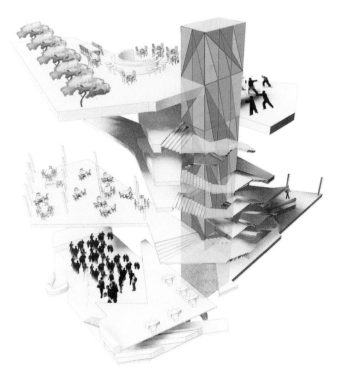

OPPOSITE
Competition watercolour study looking out under canopy.

TOP
First floor café looking out under canopy.

BOTTOM
The main stair winds around the lift shaft, Vitreous Enamel decorative artwork.

Space for Architecture

LEFT
Winding stair.

OPPOSITE
Spiral stair.

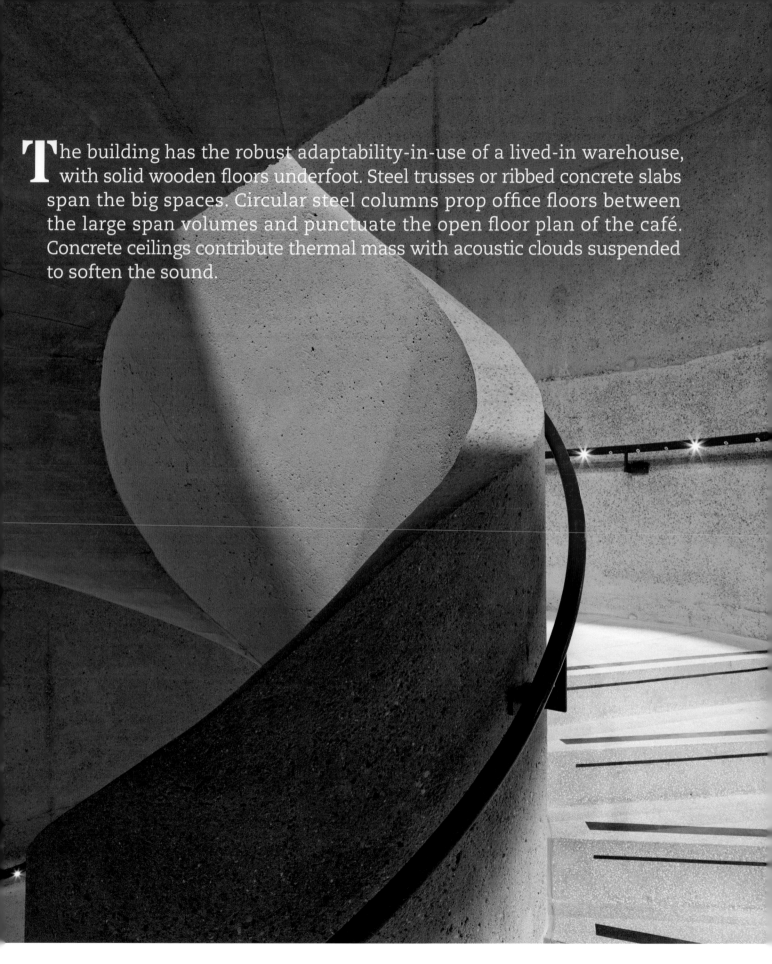

The building has the robust adaptability-in-use of a lived-in warehouse, with solid wooden floors underfoot. Steel trusses or ribbed concrete slabs span the big spaces. Circular steel columns prop office floors between the large span volumes and punctuate the open floor plan of the café. Concrete ceilings contribute thermal mass with acoustic clouds suspended to soften the sound.

TOP
Street view from
third floor.

BOTTOM
LSE Competition sketch,
London skyline.

OPPOSITE
Street view from
sixth floor.

OVERLEAF
Brick Mountain.

Future Perfect

W illiam Morris said you should speak to an audience of one as you would speak to one hundred. Recently invited to participate in a public lecture series at the National Gallery of Ireland under the heading "Designing for the Future", we found ourselves speaking to a sparsely peopled gathering about the past, about the permanence of the Pantheon and the role of the future perfect in an architect's mental make-up. We recalled two anecdotal episodes out of our life narrative to set the scene.

Campo Martio   No matter how many times you return to look out your Roman holiday hotel window, the Pantheon's portico stoically stands its ground, indifferent to your admiring gaze. The day begins at a carefully chosen spot at the usual café counter, chosen with care to allow you to divide your attentions between drinking a morning espresso and keeping the old brick elephant in clear view out of the corner of your eye. Last grappa of the evening is taken at the properly named Tempio Bar, right opposite the lit-up Pantheon, most impressively timeless at this hour, at any hour, at any time. At times like this the much-copied original reminds you, superficially, of a well-worn image of itself and, at the same time, more fundamentally, of the origins of civic architecture.

The Pantheon holds its canonical place in the architectural pantheon, its endurance impervious to the changes and continuities that have provided the conditions for its unconditional survival through two thousand years. An architectural form full of pagan history, passively resistant to Christian ritual, burial place of the divine Raphael, it is today mostly appreciated for its existential presence, the simple wonder of an ancient empty vessel wide open to the elements, suddenly made manifest to our senses through the spectacle of its oculus, by columns of solid sunlight slanting across its concrete shell or by showers of rain power-washing its sloping floor.

Brick, concrete and stone; the whole heavy structure facing north, its x axis extending out onto the public ground of the adjoining piazza, its y axis leading up into the open air of the heavens above. This was once and somehow still remains a brand new building, radical in its intentions, inventive in its construction, belonging to its place and also promising possibilities beyond its physical limits.

Epidauros   We had come to Epidauros in hope of catching an evening performance, some unspecified, hopefully surtitled, Greek tragedy. At the ticket office they apologised because, postponed due to last year's forest fires, there would be a special show tonight of Beckett's *Happy Days*. We were lucky enough to witness Fiona Shaw's Winnie struggling to maintain her optimism, buried up to her neck at the epicentre of ancient drama. Beckett's classic twentieth century theatre of the absurd, adapted to an archetypal setting, owls hooting in the trees and other sounds off, against the black starry backdrop and a rising moon. And Winnie telling herself "Oh this is a happy day, this will have been another happy day! After all. So far." We could interpret her repeated reliance on the future perfect as analogous to the way an architect has to think about time, suspended as he is, as she was, between the past and the future.

OPPOSITE
The Pantheon from
a hotel window.

The Living Present   To envisage a project having any sense of permanence in its built reality you might have to push your mind forward to an unspecified point in the imagined past of a fictional future and, from that precarious vantage point, look back over the likely lasting consequences of any actions you are about to propose in the immediate present. This is one meaning of the word project, used as a verb, to propel.

Even the grand old Pantheon must once have seemed disruptively new in ancient Rome. We have seen the archaic drama of *Happy Days* brought to new sense via an Arcadian engagement with architecture and nature. New and old are not really adequate terms to describe the purposeful vitality of architecture. The future perfect is a progressive tense, a useful position from which to fortify the proposition of a particular design, rehearse some of its more difficult parts, or perhaps seize

the moment to change your mind and start over again, to fail again, fail better. We should not be persuading ourselves into a fool's paradise of an impossibly perfect future. We should be reminding ourselves, again and again, by way of the future perfect, of the more complex dimensions of what will have been, of the imperfect reality of this continuous and living present. After all. So far.

ABOVE
The Pantheon, morning and night.

OPPOSITE
Composite functions, compatible plans connected.

Space for Architecture

Selected Works 1999–2014 We would like to acknowledge the commitment and creative contribution of the architects who worked with us on the projects selected for this book.

1999–2006 CHERRY ORCHARD SCHOOL, DUBLIN Will Dimond (associate), Jitka Leonard (project architect), Jeana Gearty, Triona Stack.

2000–2009 TIMBERYARD SOCIAL HOUSING, LIBERTIES, DUBLIN Jeana Gearty (associate/project architect), Cian Deegan, Gary Watkin, Des Cooper, Harriet Browne.

2000–2003 HOWTH HOUSE, DUBLIN Susie Carson (project architect), Rebecca Egan.

2001–2004 LEWIS GLUCKSMAN GALLERY, UNIVERSITY COLLEGE CORK Willie Carey, Andrew Morrison (project architects), Jitka Leonard, Will Dimond, Peter Carroll, Beatrix Schmidt, Kevin Donovan, Jeana Gearty.

2003–2011 LYRIC THEATRE, BELFAST Jeana Gearty (associate), Mark Grehan (project architect), Miguel Angel Santamaria, Susie Carson, Gary Watkin, Jane Larmour, Iseult O'Clery.

2004 IRELANDS' PAVILION, VENICE BIENNALE Susie Carson (project architect), Will Dimond, Willie Carey, Jeana Gearty, Elizabeth Burns.

2004–2009 IRISH LANGUAGE CULTURAL CENTRE, DERRY Willie Carey (associate), Anne-Louise Duignan (project architect), Mark Grehan, Geoff Brouder, Laura Harty.

2005–2007 KILLINEY HOUSE, DUBLIN Triona Stack (associate/project architect), Susie Carson.

2006–2008 SEÁN O'CASEY COMMUNITY CENTRE, EAST WALL, DUBLIN Laura Harty (project architect), Jitka Leonard, Geoff Brouder.

2008 THE LIVES OF SPACES, VENICE BIENNALE Jack Hogan (project architect), Jérôme Glairoux.

2009–2011 THE PHOTOGRAPHERS' GALLERY, SOHO, LONDON Willie Carey (associate), Henrik Wolterstorff (project architect), Jitka Leonard, Jane Larmour.

2009–2014 SAW SWEE HOCK STUDENT CENTRE, LONDON SCHOOL OF ECONOMICS Willie Carey (associate director), Geoff Brouder, Laura Harty, Kirstie Smeaton (project architects), Anne Louise Duignan, Gary Watkin, Mark Grehan, Ciara Reddy, Iseult O'Clery, Jeana Gearty, Henrik Wolterstorff.

2011–2018 CENTRAL EUROPEAN UNIVERSITY, BUDAPEST Mark Grehan (associate), Ciara Reddy (project architect), Geoff Brouder, Anne-Louise Duignan, Jitka Leonard, Brian Barber, Jonathan Janssens, Iseult O'Clery, Donn Holohan, Edin Gicevic, Gary Watkin.

2012 VESSEL, VENICE BIENNALE Brian Barber (project architect), Jonathan Janssens, Donn Holohan, Laura Harty, Gary Watkin.

And we would like to thank the following people for their patient help with making this particular book: Dennis Gilbert and Alice Clancy, for their perceptive photography; Laura Harty and Brian Barber, our in-house editors; Duncan McCorquodale for initiating the project and Rachel Pfleger, book designer from Artifice.

Biographies   Sheila O'Donnell and John Tuomey have worked together for more than 25 years. They have exhibited three times at the Venice Biennale. They received the RIAI Gold Medal in 2005 and have been seven times winners of the AAI Downes Medal. They have been twice shortlisted for the RIBA Lubetkin Prize, four times for the Mies van der Rohe European Award, and four times for the RIBA Stirling Prize. They both teach at University College Dublin and have lectured at schools of architecture in Europe, the UK and USA, including Harvard, Princeton, Cambridge and the AA. They were elected honorary fellows of the American Institute of Architects in 2010. They are members of Aosdána, the affiliation of Irish artists. Previous publications include *O'Donnell + Tuomey Selected Works* published by Princeton Architectural Press in 2006.

The authors in the Vessel at the Venice Biennale 2012.

© 2014 Artifice books on architecture, the architects and the authors.
All rights reserved.

Artifice books on architecture
10A Acton Street
London
WC1X 9NG

t. +44 (0)207 713 5097
f. +44 (0)207 713 8682
sales@artificebooksonline.com
www.artificebooksonline.com

Designed by Rachel Pfleger at Artifice books on architecture.
British Library Cataloguing-in-Publication Data.
A CIP record for this book is available from the British Library.

ISBN 978 1 908967 47 3

Artifice books on architecture is an environmentally responsible company.
Space for Architecture: The work of O'Donnell+Tuomey is printed on sustainably
sourced paper.

Also available:
Saw See Hock: The Realisation of the London School of Economics Student Centre
ISBN 978 1 908967 52 7